HUMAN
CAPITALISM

HUMAN CAPITALISM

❑

The Japanese Enterprise System as World Model

ROBERT S. OZAKI

Kodansha International
Tokyo • New York • London

Distributed in the United States by Kodansha America, Inc.,
114 Fifth Avenue, New York, New York, 10011.
Published by Kodansha International Ltd.,
17-14, Otowa 1-chome, Bunkyo-ku, Tokyo 112
and Kodansha America, Inc.

Printed in the United States of America.

First edition, 1991

91 92 93 94   7 6 5 4 3 2 1

Library of Congress Cataloging-in-Publication Data
Ozaki, Robert S.
Human capitalism : the Japanese enterprise system as world model /
Robert S. Ozaki. — 1st ed.
p.   cm.
Includes bibliographical references and index.
ISBN 4-7700-1549-6
1. Management—Japan—Employee participation.   2. Management—
Employee participation.   3. Industrial management—Japan.
4. Industrial management.   5. Capitalism—Japan.   6. Capitalism.
I. Title.
HD5660.J3095   1991
331'.01'12—dc20   91-8095
CIP

• • •

*The text of this book was set in Times Roman.
Composed by Folio Graphics Company, Inc.,
New York, New York.*

*Printed and bound by
R. R. Donnelley & Sons Company,
Harrisonburg, Virginia.*

TO REBECCA AND JENNIFER,
ONCE MORE WITH LOVE

CONTENTS

Preface . . . ix

Introduction . . . 1

1 The Humanistic Enterprise System . . . 6

2 Competitive Egalitarianism . . . 26

3 Between Market and Organization . . . 47

4 How Human Capitalism Evolved . . . 64

5 The Question of Culture . . . 80

6 Relationship to the Japanese-Style Management System . . . 96

7 Broader Implications . . . 112

8 Comparison with Capitalism and Socialism . . . 126

9 Previous Attempts to Reform Socialism and Capitalism . . . 141

10 The Universality of Human Capitalism . . . 158

Appendix . . . 185

Bibliography . . . 193

Index . . . 202

About the Author . . . 212

PREFACE

This book is about intangibles because it has to do with values, meaning, perception, and a way of life. It is about an enterprise that behaves more like a living organism resiliently adapting itself to changing circumstances than an impersonal business firm mechanically pursuing its objective of profit maximization. It is about companies that make a lot of money by deemphasizing their materialistic goals.

This book is about a new economic system that has evolved in a corner of the globe and that will most probably become a major trend of the future. The corner of the globe happens to be Japan. Where the phenomenon originated, however, is insignificant; the subject transcends the country and its culture.

The new economic system has worldwide implications. Many capitalistic countries in the West, including the United States, suffer from sluggish productivity gains and alienation of workers in the industrial workplace. This book shows why their root causes lie beyond the management system and how the problems may be addressed. The East European countries, liberated from the burden of centralist socialism, are now attempting to move toward capitalism with a human face. Their task is not easy, because they have no proven blueprint to guide the transition. This book offers suggestions for their success. It will provide Latin American leaders with useful ideas on how to promote their countries' economic development and growth without sacrificing equity and justice. It should help Asian nations to understand better how the Japanese economy really works, now that the Pacific Rim, under Japan's economic influence, has become the center of world production. It may even impart gentle lessons to the leaders of the communist regime in China, the most populous nation on earth, on how to end the tragic irony that the Chinese people, to prosper, must live outside their own country.

In the minds of many foreign observers there has been a contradictory image of the Japanese economy as highly competitive and yet substantially cartelized. Japanese firms seem to compete as well as cooperate with each other, at once faithfully following and blatantly violating the doctrine of Adam Smith that free-market competition is the assured way to achieve economic success. This is a paradox. If their perception is correct, Japan should have been merely an average performer in economic growth, since the positive effect of competition is cancelled out by the negative effect of its absence. Or perhaps it is the particular looking-glass worn by the foreign observers that makes it appear paradoxical. I began to ponder this question long ago.

Writing a book is a collective endeavor. Since the gestation of this book has taken a number of years, I have accumulated large debts to the many people—scholars, government economists, workers, managers, executives, students, and editors in the United States as well as in Japan—who helped me with their ideas, comments, criticisms of the manuscript, bibliographical information, empirical data, and editorial suggestions. I am particularly grateful to the following individuals for their assistance: Hiroyuki Itami, Takayuki Hazumi, Chalmers Johnson, Gerald Stoner, Shyam Kamath, John Kilgour, Kurt Leube, Douglas Orr, David St. Clair, Kazuo Tanaka, Yushiro Saito, Tetsuya Ishii, Tetsuro Sueyoshi, Cecilia Ozaki, Minato Asakawa, Mark Polizzotti, Carole De Santi, Paul De Angelis, and Kyle Dean Ono. Their views, however, do not necessarily coincide with the ones expounded in this book.

Berkeley, California

HUMAN
CAPITALISM

INTRODUCTION

A new economic system of historic importance evolved in Japan after World War II, though this fact is not yet widely recognized, let alone well understood. Neither capitalism nor socialism, it is a highly productive, people-oriented system based on the premise that human—not pecuniary or material—resources are the most vital capital with which to create and increase the wealth of nations. I have taken the liberty of calling it "human capitalism" or the "humanistic enterprise system."

There are three main grounds on which a company under human capitalism significantly differs from the traditional capitalistic firm. First, management and workers of the humanistic firm constitute an integrated group, assume primary sovereignty, and behave as if they jointly own the firm (under traditional capitalism, primary sovereignty lies in the hands of the firm's ownership and of management representing the owners', but not necessarily the workers', interests). Second, the humanistic firm both competes *and* cooperates with other firms in the context of an organized market, in contrast to the capitalistic firm, which is only supposed to compete with other firms, in a free market. Third, at the humanistic firm, management and workers substantially share decision making, the fruits of their work efforts, and information, while at the capitalistic firm these are concentrated among ownership and management. (Human capitalism definitely differs from socialism, under which the state is sovereign, the market does

1

not exist, and the firm serves as an instrument of the state's central economic planning.)

At the outset, human capitalism might appear to be counter-competitive. It explicitly emphasizes cooperation, sharing, and egalitarianism, principles that are often considered antithetical to the very idea of competition. Further, words such as *humanistic* or *people oriented* evoke a genteel organization of people uninterested in hard work and discipline, perhaps a commune inhabited by social misfits and hippies. But this is far from the truth. In reality, keen competition prevails under the humanistic enterprise system, though it is of a different sort from the capitalistic model.

Human capitalism is no more a "Japan" phenomenon than capitalism, born in eighteenth-century England, is an "English" phenomenon. It happened to evolve in postwar Japan because of the right set of circumstances at a particular time and place.

Human capitalism has been the foundation of Japan's postwar economic rebirth. It took concrete shape in the course of the nation's accelerated economic growth, and demonstrated its capacity to mobilize the productive energies of ordinary workers. At the same time, its principles are rational and universal, and therefore transferable to other countries and cultures.

It has been fashionable for Western observers to adopt a "cultural" approach to Japan. The culture model alleges that Japanese culture is significantly different from Western culture, and that the Japanese economy that functions in the context of Japanese culture must be interpreted accordingly. This model tends to confuse, rather than clarify, issues. It laxly attributes to culture anything about the Japanese economy that does not make sense in terms of the Western model (the culture-based argument not infrequently degenerates into tautology), explaining everything and nothing. It is prone to overemphasize intercultural differences and to ignore or miss universal elements. The truth of the matter is that human capitalism has little to do with traditional Japanese culture.

Every economic system—whether capitalism or socialism—is based on principles that can be expressed in abstract language. When a system is put into practice, however, it needs to be modified and adjusted to meet the expectations and requirements of a particular society. Thus managerial systems in America and Italy are not identical, though the two are capitalistic countries; and the same could be said for two socialist economies. Human capitalism has not been properly understood because it is often confused with the so-called Japanese-style management system. This system is based on the principles of human capitalism. Because Japanese firms are managed in the context of Japanese culture, these principles must be applied in a manner consistent with the particular customs and conventions of the land. Many aspects of the Japanese-style management system, therefore, are culture bound and not readily transferable elsewhere. This does not mean that human capitalism is culture specific and nontransferable. On the contrary, the universal principles of human capitalism are adaptable to varied management systems suited for different cultures.

Human capitalism was not suddenly born out of political revolution, in accordance with a well-publicized master plan. Rather, it evolved in silence, without a blueprint, through the trial and error of numerous obscure managers and workers in search of a more satisfying industrial workplace than had previously existed. It is a system on which no comprehensive treatise has thus far been written.

Why not? Because in the economic community, human capitalism is not recognized as a discrete system. Since Japan is a capitalistic country, observers naturally assume that Japanese firms act like traditional capitalistic firms. In addition, the paradigm of conventional economics is ill equipped to recognize a new system. Conventional economics presupposes only two major economic systems worthy of note: capitalism and socialism, or a mix of the two. True, these two systems are the major ones that, at least until 1989, have prevailed in the West, where the main thrust of modern economic development and growth has taken place. Human capitalism, however, is neither capitalism, socialism, nor a mixed economy in the conventional sense of the term, and many of its characteristics cannot accurately be grasped as long as one views them through the capitalism/socialism dichotomy.

Neoclassical theory of the firm occupies a large domain of Western establishment economics. An abstract modeling of capitalistic firms, the theory presents an image of the firm as an impersonal, mechanistic organization where management makes decisions for profit maximization, and faceless workers, apparently devoid of emotion, perform specialized tasks as stipulated by management. The uninitiated wonder if the theory is meant to be an accurate description of the firm as it functions in the real world or a suggested prescription of what the firm is supposed to be like. The practitioners of the theory, however, often cultivate a conditioned reflex of thought which makes anything that does not neatly fit the neoclassical framework sound odd and anomalous. The humanistic firm, while perfectly sensible in terms of its own frame of reference, does comprise elements that seem to be aberrations from a neoclassical perspective.

As we approach the close of the twentieth century, we observe a rising global sentiment for a more people-oriented economic system than either capitalism or socialism has been able to offer. Capitalism has been, and continues to be, an efficient system for producing material output but not human satisfaction in the industrial workplace, while socialism (as recent events show) has failed to be the panacea for the inherent malaise of capitalism. Theoretically consistent and practically workable, human capitalism provides a viable third way. It is of historic significance because it echoes and accentuates contemporary global sentiment, and anticipates the type of economic system likely to gain currency in the twenty-first century.

When Adam Smith wrote his classic *An Inquiry into the Nature and Causes of the Wealth of Nations* (commonly known as *The Wealth of Nations*) in 1776, he was expounding the universal principles of a dynamic new economic system (later to be named capitalism) that happened to evolve in eighteenth-century England and became a world system in subsequent centuries. It is my contention that something comparable to the birth of classical capitalism has taken place two hundred years later in an opposite corner of the globe. This book is my modest attempt to identify and discuss the newly emerged system.

1

THE HUMANISTIC ENTERPRISE SYSTEM

❑

The Nature of the Firm

Human economic activity does not take place in a vacuum. Every nation operates under an economic system composed of those laws, rules, and regulations that jointly determine how the nation allocates its resources toward production, distribution, and consumption of goods and services. In one way or another, such factors as the nature of available technology, the scarcity or abundance of specific resources, and prevailing values and expectations define and condition the properties of a given system. Along with shifts of the economic environment over time, the economic system, too, is bound to change sooner or later.

History indicates two basic ways in which a new economic system comes into existence. It can evolve on its own, replacing the old system because it appears to be more rational and efficient in solving the nation's economic problems (the spontaneous emergence of capitalism in eighteenth-century England is a case in point). Or a reformist thinker with enough talent and fervor (Karl Marx, for instance) may construct an abstract model; he and his followers, via a popular revolutionary movement, eventually succeed in imposing the new system on the ruins of the old regime.

But regardless of its origin, every economic system is more than a collection of laws and regulations. It represents values and a way of life. It comes with a set of philosophical and ideological principles that define its overall character. Thus we can identify capitalism as a system based on the values of individual liberties, competition, and a firm belief in private-property rights. In contrast, socialism is a system that upholds collective welfare, economic equity, and public ownership of the means of production.

These abstract principles in turn determine the general characteristics of the respective enterprise system—the set of institutional rules and conventions by which a representative firm, under that system, organizes itself, allocates its internal resources, makes strategic and operational decisions, behaves as a grouping of people, and interacts with other firms. To varying degrees, a firm's practice may depart from theory, but still remains within the general context of its corresponding economic system. One would not expect many firms in the Soviet Union to behave like typical American ones, or vice versa.

In the case of contemporary Japan, the economic system is neither socialism—as Japan does not practice economic planning, and the state does not own the means of production—nor, properly speaking, capitalism. While the bulk of the nation's output is produced through a private, free, fiercely competitive market, looking more closely we observe that the usual behavior of representative Japanese firms (large, highly efficient ones that operate in the most advanced sectors of the economy and constitute the core of Japan's business establishment) deviates from the norm of capitalism to such an extent that it becomes misleading or even inaccurate to describe Japan as capitalistic.

It is hard, for example, to determine who owns those firms. The bulk of stocks is held institutionally rather than individually, and firms extensively practice mutual stock-holding: Company A holds shares of Company B's stock and Company C's, B owns shares of A's and C's, and so on. If corporate ownership determines control over the firm, then we must describe this as a system in which everybody controls everyone else—which is to say, nobody controls anybody. The firms' substantial mutual ownership makes management of each firm almost completely free of capitalists' intervention from outside.

7

Management and workers identify with their firm and with each other. They act as though they own the firm where they work. To them, the notion that shareholders are the legal owners of their firm is a meaningless technicality. Management does not perceive itself as representing the owners' interests. Both management and workers view themselves as one group jointly striving for the prosperity and growth of their firm, that is, for themselves.

Firms widely practice the principles of sharing. The rights, responsibilities, risks, information, and fruits of their efforts are substantially shared between and among management and workers. Thus decision making is diffused and consensual. Each year's "value added" (net revenue), large or small, is sizably distributed to workers under a variable wage system. The gap between the top executive salary and the lowest starting wage is incomparably narrower than in America. There are few institutional arrangements within the firm (such as parking space reserved for managers, or executive dining rooms) that facilitate or accentuate class consciousness between management and workers or between blue- and white-collar workers.

The firms both compete and cooperate with other firms. They often operate in the context of an organized market: namely, one firm enters into a long-term cooperative relationship with another firm, for mutual gain. The firms form enterprise groups, each group being a loose, flexible coalition of firms whose goal is mutual support. There is intense intragroup collaboration, while keen competition prevails *between* enterprise groups.

These major traits of typical Japanese firms stand in sharp contrast to the behavioral characteristics of their American counterparts. Although no two companies are identical, the representative firms in any given country reveal a set of common, generalizable attributes, which are sufficiently different from those of firms in other countries to allow meaningful comparisons without gross distortion of the truth.

The typical American firm is an institution corporately owned by shareholders. Whenever they deem it desirable, the

8

shareholders, institutional or individual, exercise their power as owners of the firm in matters of corporate mergers and take-overs, firing of unsatisfactory executives, etc. Management represents capitalists' interest, not workers'. The latter are "employees" hired by the firm for their skills, in exchange for fixed wages. As a general principle, workers feel little loyalty to the firm; they may be fired at the whim of management, or they may quit in search of a better job. Managers, too, readily go elsewhere for higher compensation.

The decision-making rights are concentrated in the hands of management. The vertical command system is the norm, the participatory or consensual system the exception. So-called "profit-sharing" plans are practiced by a fair number of firms, but more often than not represent tokenism rather than a significant sharing of the fruits of the company. The top executive salary is usually disproportionately higher than the lowest wage of a production worker.

The firm operates primarily in the context of a free, rather than organized, market. Under law, the firm is expected only to compete with other firms. A firm that attempts to cooperate with another runs the risk of being charged with antitrust violations. It is the fundamental assumption of traditional American antimonopoly philosophy that in the marketplace, if not in other spheres of human activity, only competition promotes efficiency, and interfirm cooperation of any sort is inimical to the public interest and economic welfare of the nation.

One might object that these differences are not substantial enough to warrant calling Japan's economic system anything other than capitalism — particularly since a private market economy does prevail there. But capitalism, as the word suggests, is a system in which capital is valued most among all factors of production, and it is therefore those who own and provide capital who exercise sovereignty. The organization of the capitalistic firm, and the roles of management and workers therein, are the logical consequences of such an orientation.

Under the Japanese system, this capital orientation is largely replaced by people orientation. The system places primary sovereignty in management and workers who produce the firm's output, actually and directly. This system did not exist in prewar Japan, but evolved after World War II. It has proven to be a productive system, as evinced by Japan's economic successes over the last several decades (Tables I and II in Appendix).

The Japanese system embraces a humanistic economic philosophy, based on three propositions: (1) human resources are the most important factor of production and are the ultimate origin of the market value of all goods produced; (2) people, unlike nonhuman resources, are intellectual (intelligence-carrying) beings in that they are capable of thinking, analyzing, inventing, innovating, and developing information vital for the creation of wealth; and (3) people are psychological (emotional) beings whose productivity may rise or fall depending on whether they are motivated or demoralized by their work environment. These three principles—in reality obvious truths—define what we call "human capitalism."

Under capitalism, the firm is in essence a house of outsiders. Those inside it (managers and workers) are transients who must be ready to leave any day. From outside, ownership exerts its power over the affairs of the house, subject to the countervailing power of another outside force, the union. Under socialism, economic power is concentrated in the state. The typical socialistic firm is a component of the planned economy, a means of realizing goals designed at the top. Although in theory workers own and control their firms, in reality the state exercises its power over activities of the firms through implementation of official economic plans. Management and workers serve the interest of the state (just as Western management serves the owners). The workers do not participate in management of the firm and are not allowed to organize a Western-style union, since, in the presumed absence of class struggle under socialism, such a union would be a contradiction.

Neither model applies to the working of the humanistic enterprise. Under human capitalism, the concept of private corporate ownership is blurred. The state does not own the means of production. Management is almost totally free of owners' influence. The market for both executives and workers is substantially internalized: both groups stay with the same firm most of their working lives, and executives are typically recruited from within ranks in the same firm. Managerial decision making is diffused, consensual, and participatory. In other words, the humanistic firm is free of outsider influences, and its management and workers make decisions independently and autonomously, controlling their own destiny.

Any firm has to cope with materialistic, intellectual, and psychological concerns. Materialistic concerns pertain to production and marketing of goods and realization of profits. Intellectual concerns are the knowledge, information, and intelligence required to produce goods efficiently and profitably. Physical and intellectual resources alone, however, are not sufficient to achieve the firm's objectives. The psychological motivation of the work force also has great bearing on the firm's productivity.

The traditional capitalistic firm tends tacitly to rank the relative importance of these three categories of problems. Profit making, the materialistic function of the firm, is generally considered most important. Everything else is understood to be a means of achieving that end. Intellectual and psychological concerns are not so much ignored as underplayed, and assume secondary roles relative to profit maximization. Human and nonhuman factors of production are treated as equally dispensable inputs. Anyone in the firm—workers and managers alike—may be dismissed in the name of improving the firm's profit. Management starts to worry about psychological problems only if and when a decline of the firm's productivity due to workers' demoralization becomes visible.

The ethos of humanistic management is more holistic than that of its capitalistic counterpart. The three categories of management problems are neither separated nor ranked by relative significance. Rather, they are grasped jointly as inseparable elements of the whole. Management does not view the work force as a mere means of profit making, but perceives the firm as an organic group of thinking and feeling beings working together for long-term prosperity and security. Workers are seen as the vital asset (human capital) generating values for the firm, instead of faceless inputs whose costs are to be minimized in pursuit of maximum profits. Ironically, this relative deemphasis of the materialistic goal of profit making actually seems to enhance the firm's prospect for realizing that goal.

Joint Management-Worker Sovereignty

Every organization must decide who should hold the authority to make important decisions about its affairs. In the context of a private enterprise system, it seems reasonable to say that those who contribute most to the value of the firm by providing its resources, and who at the same time assume the greatest risks in case of business failure, should hold primary sovereignty. Rights without responsibilities and responsibilities without rights are equally illogical. In practice, this principle leads to varied applications.

If a person invests his or her own money in a venture, and is the sole owner/manager/worker of the firm, that person alone, needless to say, should be the sovereign. If a family totally owns the firm managed and operated only by its members, the family or the family head would be the natural holder of the rights to control it. In the case of a small business wholly owned and managed by one person with the help of a handful of hired hands doing simple, unskilled, routine jobs, it is sensible to assume that most sovereignty rests with that person.

In the age of classical capitalism, determining who should be the sovereign was relatively easy and simple. In the late eighteenth and early nineteenth centuries, the representative firm was a little shop or a small firm owned and managed by one or a few capitalists together with a small group of workers who did not contribute capital to the enterprise. Then, capital was scarce and vital, labor cheap and abundant. Capitalists added most to the value of the output of the firm by supplying the important resource. They would lose most if the business failed. Without ambiguity, the capitalists were sovereign. Capitalism was a rational system in the context of the time.

With the coming of large corporations in the twentieth century, the issue of sovereignty becomes more complicated. Let us consider a representative large capitalistic firm in contemporary America. There are four main groups affiliated with the firm: stockholders, creditors, management, and workers. (The government indirectly affects the firm through taxation, subsidies, and regulations; but we shall keep the government out of the picture, since under capitalism government cannot directly participate in the firm's internal affairs.) The above four groups all add value to the company's output to different degrees, and at the same time bear varied risks related to their affiliation with the firm.

Capitalists (stockholders) offer equity capital with which the firm acquires machines, tools, and equipment. The firm cannot operate without these means of production, so their contribution to the firm is undeniable. They are rewarded with dividends, which may be large, small, or zero depending on business conditions and management policy, and with capital gains, which may come as a matter of sheer luck or as a consequence of wise investment. If the company goes bankrupt, capitalists lose all of their investments. They may also suffer capital losses when the firm's condition deteriorates. Capitalists, however, can reduce their risks by diversifying their investments instead of concentrating their capital in one or a few firms.

The firm borrows money from institutional or individual creditors as necessary to finance its operations. To the extent that its activity depends on external loans, the creditors' contribution is self-evident. Creditors receive obligatory interest on their outstanding loans, and have neither capital gains nor capital losses. In the event of a major business failure they bear the risk of probably not being able to recover their money fully. As do capitalists, creditors have the option of spreading their risks by lending to many different companies.

The corporation is run by hired professional managers rather than by capitalists themselves. Managers are compensated for their work with salaries, bonuses, and other benefits. If their firm fails, they are faced with a myriad of risks: the loss of high salaries, benefits, privileges; the economic and psychological costs of unemployment; the loss of reputation and the likelihood of a lower salary on the next job; the high legal fees needed to ward off stockholders' class-action suits against them, and the like. These risks may be considerably offset by "golden parachutes," consisting of generous, contractually determined severance pay and other benefits.

Workers, by far the largest group affiliated with the firm, exchange their skills for wages. If the firm fails, workers must assume the risks of losing their wages, of absorbing the costs of unemployment and the search for a new job, and of possibly accepting a lower wage on the next job. These costs might be alleviated by various kinds of unemployment compensation. Unlike investors, however, workers cannot diversify their risks by working for numerous firms at once.

The preceding survey reveals that all four groups make contributions to the firm and assume risks of one kind or another and, further, that it is impossible to calculate with precision the extent to which each group adds value to the company's output. Total value added is a synthetic, cumulative outcome of contributions made by the four groups, and each group's relative significance can only be estimated in a given situation.

If we are to apply the principle that "the more contribution one makes and the higher the risk one bears, the more sovereignty one should assume," sovereignty must be assigned variedly to all groups rather than to any single one. In fact, this is done. Management has the power to make major managerial decisions, though they are subject to capitalists' approval. Large creditors can threaten to withdraw funds or to refuse to issue new credits. Workers may use the "voice" of their union to restrain the abuse of management power.

Under capitalism, however, capitalists hold disproportionately more power than all other groups. Capitalist sovereignty made perfect sense in past centuries, in the age of small shops, each owned and managed by one or two people. Today it is still perfectly legal for a handful of capitalists to manipulate their stock-ownership rights in order to dissolve, merge, or take over a large corporation, causing a mass layoff of its employees—even though the capitalists' initial investment value might be a small fraction of the corportion's present total asset value. In the feudal period the king, because he was the king, could do almost anything with his land and subjects. Such a rule strikes modern man as absurd, but isn't it equally absurd to endow a few capitalists with the supreme power to adversely affect the lives of thousands of other individuals?

Under human capitalism, the same four groups exist, but they play different roles, so that the distribution of power among them becomes quite another matter.

Thanks to interfirm mutual stockholding and a relatively heavy reliance on debt financing, the role of capitalists is reduced to a point of insignificance. There are few individual capitalists owning enough shares to be able to control the major firms. Management does pay attention to individual stockholders by offering them modest dividends, but in fact it disdains dividends as unwelcome costs to the firm that are not, unlike interest, tax deductible. Management, in effect, is almost completely free from the influence of capitalists as a group.

The firm heavily borrows from large city banks that typically belong to the same enterprise as the firm does. While the banks contribute substantially to the firm's value creation as providers of major credits, they are the ones that will suffer if the firm fails. They cannot afford to interfere with the management of the borrowing firm in a manner that will benefit them at the firm's expense. The power they exercise over the firm's affairs as creditors, therefore, is friendly and supportive rather than hostile and interventionist.

That leaves two groups, management and workers, who in

the context of the humanistic enterprise system constitute one integrated group. The market for both labor and executives is *internalized,* limiting their interfirm mobility. Managers and workers view their firm as of, by, and for them, and jointly strive toward accumulation of intrafirm human capital. Their compensations are largely adjusted to the level of their firm-specific skills and know-how, and rise with the number of years of company service. While they are the major contributors to the firm's worth, they are also heavy risk-bearers. If the company fails, compelling them to search for new jobs elsewhere, they will find it difficult to find comparable jobs — since a humanistic firm as a rule does not hire workers from another humanistic firm — and they will probably have to accept considerably lower wages at other firms where the labor market is not internalized (Table III in Appendix).

To describe the humanistic firm adequately, we need a new expression. Management and workers of the humanistic firm are one group sharing a common interest. The word *workers* is inadequate, as it connotes a group apart from management. *Employees* is improper, as it suggests a group of passive individuals with little autonomy, hired by and working for the company. *Affiliates* and *associates* are inappropriate, since they sound as if they do not really belong to the firm. Unfortunately, the English language at present offers no single word that describes "management *and* workers" as one group. In contrast to capitalist sovereignty under traditional capitalism and state sovereignty under socialism, management and workers under human capitalism who actually are inside the company and run it through consensual and participatory management hold the primary power to control their own firm. We will call it "joint management-worker sovereignty."

Ownership and Control

Capitalism is an economic system based on the principle of private-property ownership according to which a person who privately owns a piece of property holds the legitimate right to control the use of it. Under capitalism, capitalists own the firm, i.e., the physical, nonhuman means of production, but not the human beings who work at the firm. Managers and workers, human components of the firm, are free individuals in the sense that they can exit from the firm anytime if they so desire.

Capitalists also have total claim on the net revenue of the firm. The rationale of this claim is arguable, however. Goods, bearing market value, are produced by machines, but only if and when the machines are operated by human workers. Both machines and people add value to the output, so owners should equitably share that added value. What is the equitable share for workers?

The neoclassical answer is that they are getting their fair share as long as they receive market wages. If workers demand more than market wages, they are said to be "exploiting" capitalists! Under classical capitalism, in the age of scarce capital and cheap and abundant labor, the capitalistic institution of ownership and control of the corporation tended to allow capitalists to get richer while the masses of workers remained poor, if not poorer. In the contemporary industrial economy, workers at a capitalistic company attempt to enlarge their share of the pie by organizing a union and demanding, through collective bargaining, higher wages than market rates.

The capitalistic institution of ownership and control makes perfect sense as long as we are dealing with a small family business, where ownership and management are one and the same, and consequently there is no conflict of interest between the two. The theory of contemporary capitalism assumes that the rationality of the institution equally applies to large corporations. The owners serve as outside overseers of the firm's management. They exercise their power to purge incompetent and lax executives, and to initiate corporate restructuring, mergers, takeovers, and the like, so that the firms they own will be efficient and profitable. As a result the firms prosper, as does the nation's economy. In reality, however, this may not be the case.

Contemporary capitalists typically are not insiders involved in the affairs of the firm they "own." They are interested in the company only to the extent that it serves their own interest. At a sign of unprofitability, they have the option of selling their shares and investing their money in another firm. Understandably, they are interested in short-run maximization of the firm's profit; the executives who opt for long-term growth at the expense of short-term profits run the risk of losing their positions. The capitalists' objective also entails compensating people inside the corporation as little as possible. So there is an institutionalized disharmony of interest between the capitalists on one hand, and management and workers on the other.

An individual will predictably be motivated when he assumes rights and responsibilities for his conduct. The contemporary firm is a grouping of many individuals. For it to behave like a highly motivated individual, it must, freely and independently of outside interference, be able to make its own decisions toward maximization of its own gains, and at the same time it must take responsibility for the consequences of its failure.

There are different ways to construct a firm so that it can control its own destiny and in effect become a well-motivated quasi-person. A worker-owned and -managed producer-cooperative-type firm is one alternative. A firm that totally avoids equity financing (issuing and selling shares of stock) and instead relies substantially on debt financing (borrowing from banks) is another, though in this case a major creditor may start to act like a quasi-owner of the firm and intervene with its management. The third option would be to restrict equity financing to issuance of preferred stock, so that the capitalists, devoid of voting rights, own the firm but cannot control it.

The humanistic firm has enabled itself to behave like a motivated individual by separating ownership from control through mutual corporate stockholding, an extensive reliance on debt financing, and (more recently) the use of accumulated retained earnings. Management and workers form one group, exercising joint sovereignty and sharing a common interest. The firm's gain is their gain. Given the internalized nature of the human-resources market, however, they must pay a high price if their firm fails.

The ethos of the humanistic firm requires new thinking about the very concept of ownership and control. Ownership of the humanistic firm is clearly not public in the socialist sense, nor is it purely private in the capitalist sense. It is not somewhere in between, either, and cannot be well articulated under the dichotomy of public versus private ownership. The members of the humanistic firm do not perceive their firm to be owned by stockholders. They may not legally own it, yet it belongs to them, as they occupy the firm and operate its facilities. One may argue that this is an instance of usufruct and that they are usufructuaries. These terms are not satisfactory, however, since *usufruct* implies that the property one is authorized to use is privately owned by someone else, whereas the members of the humanistic firm do not consider themselves to be leasing their firm from capitalists. In the absence of the appropriate expression, we might say that they are the quasi-private owners of their firm.

If this new concept of nonownership and control were observed only among tribesmen of the Amazon rain forests, we would be tempted to brush it aside as a curious anthropological anomaly. But in truth, this concept is what underlies the enterprise system responsible for producing the world's second largest GNP. It is important to note that human capitalism is not confined to industrial firms. The majority of well-established, leading corporations in Japan, operating in all fields (manufacturing, banking, insurance, trading, communication, transportation, mass media, etc.), practice the basic principles of joint management-worker sovereignty, nonownership and control, and sharing. Quasi-private ownership of the humanistic firm offers an alternative to both private-property rights and public ownership of the means of production.

In the United States much has been said about the separation of corporate ownership from control. In the early part of this century, large corporations began to emerge. Given their size, the original capitalists and their family members could no longer personally manage their firms, and so they hired professional managers. Hence the idea of separation of ownership from control. This phenomenon, however, needs to be interpreted with caution. In contemporary American capitalism, managers might handle the company's day-to-day affairs; yet they do not fully control it, inasmuch as their major strategic decisions (and to a large extent their tenure) are subject to the concurrence of stockholders.

The humanistic enterprise system evolved as a de facto system within the framework of capitalism, which suggests that it is possible to build it in other capitalistic countries without a revolution or sweeping legal reforms. The edifice of capitalism still stands in contemporary Japan. The humanistic firm has a chairman of the board, a board of directors, chief executive officer, senior executive vice-presidents, stockholders' meetings, and all the rest. It's in the way they function that we see the difference.

The president is the highest-level decision-maker of the firm. The board of directors does not oversee his conduct, as the majority of the board members are usually senior supervisors of the same firm and subordinate to the president. It is inconceivable that subordinates who selected the president for his talent and ability would vote to dismiss him without overwhelming evidence of his malperformance. The chairman of the board of directors is probably an elderly former president, a symbolic figure. A typical stockholders' meeting is a mockery of the spirit of traditional capitalism. It is held because it is a legal requirement under the formal system. Institutional shareholders, i.e., corporations affiliated with the firm, have already turned in their proxy ballots all blank. Senior directors on the stage perform the ritual of reciting brief statements on the company's accomplishments and prospects for the new year. The meeting is usually over in twenty minutes or so.

If the president makes gross errors, he will resign under collective pressure from his management and workers. The stockholders' meeting will still be brief. If individual share-holders start to raise hell on the floor, they will immediately be shut up and removed from the room by professional bouncers called *sokaiya*.

Sharing

Forming an organization assumes that a group of individuals, acting together as its members, can achieve a certain goal better and more effectively than those individuals can when acting separately. Such an attempt to generate synergy is aimed at creating a whole greater than the sum of its parts.

Since every organization is a grouping of people, all organizations—whether their objectives are economic or political—are social organizations, regardless of working principles that may or may not emphasize that fact. The firm, too, is at once an economic and a social organization.

In practice, the capitalistic firm is understood to be primarily, if not exclusively, an economic organization whose objective is to make profits. Each employee is given, and is expected to serve, a certain specified function in exchange for an associated compensation. An employee with marginal or substandard performance will be demoted to a lower function or laid off. The worker's association with the firm is purely an economic one, the firm being a means of maximizing his or her pecuniary income. The firm in turn perceives each worker as an input, a means of maximizing its profits. The firm is a collection of functions to which people are fit. People may come and go, but the collection of functions stays intact.

Economic functionalism is one mode of operating the firm. It can be rational and efficient if the nature of production permits a high degree of division of labor and workers are satisfied with their purely functional roles. Functionalism is also the antithesis of the principle of sharing. Workers are expected to concentrate on their functions, and not to cooperate with other workers or share knowledge and know-how. Workers' mutual cooperation would break down the system of division of labor, and thence hamper the firm's economic efficiency.

Another alternative is to approach the firm as primarily a social organization. Suppose a group of ten like-minded men and women establish a workers'-cooperative-type firm selling fruits and vegetables. They share profits, losses, work, and everything else. Their concern is social efficiency in maximizing their mutual happiness and psychic welfare.

Cheese Board in Berkeley, California, is an example of the firm that is primarily a social organization. Very popular among local cheese lovers, it is a cooperative run by a group of men and women who believe in communalism as a way of life. Making money is not their main concern. They regularly donate a portion of their collective income to various social causes. When a member was killed in a car accident, they closed the store for one entire week to mourn the partner's death.

We cannot judge a priori if a socially efficient firm will also be economically efficient. Social and economic efficiencies of the firm can be substitutes or complements of one another. It is hard to imagine that people interested more in psychic rewards than in pecuniary gains will drive themselves hard in pursuit of profits. At the same time, it is conceivable that workers' happiness and satisfaction in a socially efficient firm will serve as a powerful motivating force for them to work hard spontaneously, resulting incidentally in good earnings. Similarly, too much emphasis on economic efficiency may lead to alienation of workers and, ironically, to economic inefficiency.

Human capitalism explicitly recognizes that the firm is an economic as well as social organization. It is clearly an economic organization, since its central goal is to make money. It is also a social organization, because it consists of human beings with feelings and emotions. Human capitalism affirms the obvious: that economic and social aspects of human activity in the firm are organically integrated, that one cannot be treated apart from the other, and that the firm cannot be economically efficient unless workers are well motivated and satisfied with their work.

How can the workers be psychologically satisfied in the course of pursuing the economic objective of the firm? By substantially sharing among its members all the benefits and costs of belonging to the firm. In the work environment, the sense of equal and fair treatment is vital to motivate individuals. A person who feels unfairly treated in one way or another will easily be demoralized. Yet the rule of absolute equality, whereby everybody is entitled to exactly the same reward irrespective of one's effort or output, will have a disincentive effect. Under such a rule all workers, motivated or not, will put in as little effort as possible. Both extreme inequality and absolute equality are counterproductive, and somewhere in between is the optimal level of equality that will maximize the collective productivity of workers. The humanistic firm tries to achieve that optimal level.

Thus the value added by the members to the firm's output is equitably distributed among themselves. The salary gap between top and bottom is strikingly modest by American standards. At the humanistic firm in contemporary Japan the top executive's after-tax salary is only about six times as large as the lowest starting salary of a newly recruited worker. The scene, familiar in America, of the chief executive officer collecting $1 million annual salary plus bonus while a production worker down below receives fifteen dollars an hour is totally inconceivable to, and would utterly demoralize, members of the humanistic firm.

In effect, workers of the humanistic firm are under a flexible wage system. Each worker's total compensation mainly consists of a regular salary and semiannually distributed bonuses, the latter flexibly adjusted to the firm's profit each year. They can be very large in good years, as large as four or five months' worth of regular salary (Table IV in Appendix). Thus pecuniary rewards are shared in two ways: through a relatively egalitarian salary scale, and by way of a substantial profit-sharing scheme that makes workers' total compensations variable over time.

Human capitalism assumes that one's motivation is enhanced when one shares responsibility and participates in the decision-making process. The humanistic firm practices the consensual, participatory management system. Management does not make key decisions unilaterally and impose them on workers. In the humanistic firm everyone is expected and encouraged to formulate and express opinions, ideas, suggestions, and criticisms. Decision making is often bottom up, and consensus building among all workers is always a chief concern of management.

Not only pecuniary rewards and responsibilities but also costs of membership are to be shared. The humanistic firm copes with recession in a manner considerably different than that of its capitalistic counterpart. When demand for the firm's output starts to fall, capitalistic management responds by laying off redundant workers. In the name of economic efficiency, this is a legitimate and legal act. The uninhibited layoff policy reminds the dismissed workers that they are no less dispensable than any other resources used by the firm.

In contrast, the humanistic firm follows a minimum layoff policy as a way of sharing the pain of hard times. Come recession, top executives' salaries are cut first, followed by reduction of middle managers' and workers' compensation. Work hours are decreased so workers can share the remaining jobs. Surplus labor in one department is transferred to another in the firm where demand remains strong. Workers may be sent, on a temporary basis, to other firms belonging to the same enterprise group. Production for inventory buildup is continued as long as possible. Redundant workers may receive special training or perform extra maintenance and repair work.

Amid the oil crisis in the early 1970s world demand for tankers collapsed, plunging the Japanese shipbuilding industry into deep recession. Yet there were no mass layoffs in the industry, as surplus shipbuilding workers were transferred to affiliated car-manufacturing firms that were booming thanks to the increased world demand for small, fuel-efficient automobiles. During the same period Toyo Kogyo in Hiroshima, the maker of Mazda cars, was on the verge of bankruptcy, having lost a huge gamble on the quiet but fuel-inefficient rotary engine. The company speedily trained a large number of its redundant production workers in sales and assigned them to Mazda showrooms and beyond, instead of laying them off outright.

The burden sharing is often practiced by the Japanese firms operating overseas. HMC (Hitachi Magnetics Corporation) in Michigan, a former division of General Electric and maker of special magnets for automobiles, was hard hit by a recession in late 1974, with a twenty-five-percent drop of its sales. The Hitachi management did not unilaterally lay off workers. Instead, after close consultations with the union (UAW), it presented the three-option plan for the workers to vote on: (1) layoff of twenty-five percent of the work force; (2) adoption of a four-days-a-week work schedule with no layoff; and (3) adoption of a three-weeks-a-month work schedule with no layoff. With a majority vote the workers amicably accepted the third alternative.

We now move to examine in the next chapter other significant aspects of the humanistic enterprise system: the internalized labor market, decentralized decision making, the incentive system, participative management, and the enterprise union.

2

COMPETITIVE
EGALITARIANISM

❏

The Internalized Labor Market

According to conventional Western economics, interfirm labor mobility is good for the nation's economy because it better allocates human resources and hence increases productivity nationwide. Workers may not be fully effective in the jobs they presently hold; if so, they can improve their productivity by moving to take up more suitable jobs elsewhere.

Not all labor mobility, of course, is of this sort. Some workers leave their jobs because they have been fired or laid off; in either case, it is doubtful that their next jobs will make them more productive. Similarly, one would not expect the outputs of born drifters to increase steadily over time as they meander from one job to another. Nonetheless, conventional economics assumes that labor mobility generally enhances productivity.

The representative capitalistic firm meets its personnel requirements mainly by hiring individuals from the external, competitive labor market. Workers have the freedom to accept or reject a job offer, while the firm may hire or fire them according to its needs for their services. The external labor market would be a rational and efficient scheme to fulfill the firm's demand for personnel if the nature of production consistently allowed a high degree of division of labor, and the jobs to be performed were always simple and routine.

The representative humanistic firm, in contrast, relies on a substantially internalized labor market. Workers are expected to stay with the same firm over a long period of time (Table V in Appendix). The system reduces interfirm mobility, and therefore (if we were to follow the wisdom of conventional economics) it should have a decreasing effect on overall productivity. But the internalized labor market has certain advantages over the external labor market, and, depending on circumstances, the former can actually be a more effective means to raise the firm's productivity than the latter.

One fundamental characteristic of human workers (as opposed to machines) is that over time their productivity can be raised through training. Formally or informally, workers can learn skills, knowledge, and know-how from others, and can become capable of producing more as well as performing progressively more difficult and differentiated skills. Human workers are also able to form teams and closely cooperate with each other in order to make their group output larger than the sum of their separate outputs.

If required skills are largely firm specific, rather than generally and easily transferable to different firms, and if the nature of production and technology demands collaborative efforts among workers, the internalized labor market provides a strategic advantage. In the external labor market, workers are expected to acquire skills on their own, which may or may not be applicable to specific firms. The skill each worker possesses may be his or her only asset. Rationally, one hesitates to teach one's skill to other workers, since this would make one's asset less scarce and lower its market value. In principle, therefore, the external labor market both inhibits firm-specific skill formation, and discourages cooperative efforts between workers.

The humanistic firm, engaged in the production of differentiated products with the use of advanced and complex technology, relies on its internalized labor pool as the effective way to build a firm-specific stock of human capital. This "human capital" provides the firm with what we might call its invisible assets (as opposed to such visible assets as machines and equipment): pertinent knowledge, information, technical know-how, learning capacity, a sense of coordination, and the like. This cohesive bundle of invisible assets can only be developed and nurtured within the firm; it cannot be acquired ready-made from outside.

Here is an example: The basic technology involved in producing word processors is the same for Toshiba and Matsushita. But the two companies have developed and rely on different production systems in combining and integrating man, machine, and equipment. Particular techniques, know-how, methods, and the art of intrafirm coordination and communication at Toshiba are subtly differentiated from those at Matsushita. Therefore, if a Toshiba worker with three years of experience in electronics moves to Matsushita, his productivity will significantly drop relative to his Matsushita counterpart because of his unfamiliarity with Matsushita's production system.

Assuming that the qualified workers are persuaded to stay with the firm for a long time, the firm can take full advantage of the internalized labor market. It will spend a good deal on in-house training of workers toward accumulation of firm-specific skills with reasonable assurance of a positive return on its investment in human capital. With a constant group of workers, the firm can plan and execute a systematic, well-coordinated training program: a worker is first trained for job A, then moves on to job B, C, D, and so on, gradually assuming more difficult and complex assignments.

In the internalized market, workers operate as members of a team. They compete for promotions and higher pay, and are evaluated on the basis both of their individual productivity and of their ability to cooperate with other members of the team in enhancing group productivity. Job rotation is the norm; each worker cultivates a sense of the interrelatedness of different functions and a holistic perception of the entire production process. The team approach encourages transfer of knowledge and know-how. Workers learn from each other, and senior members of the team do not hesitate to teach junior members new skills in the absence of a concern that the new skills, so transmitted, will threaten the senior member's position in the firm. On the contrary, it is a large part of the senior member's responsibility to transfer skills to the less experienced members.

The central reason to rely on the internalized labor market is so that the well-integrated, internal work force, together with the visible assets, can produce significantly more than a firm that draws its supply of labor from the external market. Working in the context of the internalized labor market, however, has certain costs: Workers give up their freedom of mobility. Of course, they may move from one firm to another as they wish, but the skills they acquired at the first firm would largely be nontransferable to the second. Nontransferability of their firm-specific skills also implies that if a firm goes bankrupt, its workers will suffer a heavy loss of real income.

In order to persuade workers to remain, the firm must therefore offer benefits that more than offset these costs. These consist primarily of higher wages than are earnable elsewhere, and long-term employment security. The internalized work force enhances the firm's productivity, and the resultant greater value added is distributed to workers as higher wages. As a means of further motivating workers to stay with the firm, the wage scale is adjusted so that the compensation, to a significant extent, is an increasing function of length of service. Beginning wages are relatively low as the firm absorbs the initial costs of training. Over time, wages steadily rise as the worker accumulates firm-specific skills. Retirement benefits also increase with time. A premature exit from the firm means the loss of a large potential income; accordingly, workers commit themselves to long-term employment.

If the firm is a monopoly operating with an internalized labor market, the workers may be tempted to exploit the firm's monopoly position by demanding an ever-increasing share of the profit, to the point of earning wages disproportionately higher than market rates. This, however, will not happen in a competitive market environment. As long as interfirm competition prevails, the internalized labor market cannot be a totally isolated world in which the workers may complacently enjoy higher wages than are earnable elsewhere. Thanks to the synergy of the integrated work force, the internalized workers can collect high wages. But if their wages become excessive, the firm's competitiveness will weaken, threatening the welfare of everyone in the firm. Interfirm competition thus serves as a restraining force against self-destructive developments from within the internalized labor market.

Decision Making

For the firm to function properly, an effective system of decision making must prevail. For a self-employed individual, decision making is simple and straightforward. If the self-employed person makes a good decision and executes it correctly, his/her business should prosper. Similarly, decision making as such creates no particular problems for a minifirm of a few partners who understand each other perfectly. In all likelihood they do not even need a formal system: each partner knows exactly what the others are doing. The principle of "give and take" is taken for granted—after all, a partnership whose members refuse to cooperate makes little sense.

As we move from the self-employed or a small partnership to a larger firm, decision making becomes increasingly difficult and complex. Bearing in mind that the firm, a collection of many individuals, is the basic unit of production and competition, we realize that the ideal is to construct one that behaves as if it were a well-motivated self-employed person. With a large number of workers, this is easier said than done. Information may get lost or misdirected. Correct decisions made by someone may be misunderstood and miscarried by someone else. The large firm thus faces a question: What sort of system of decision making will be most effective in pursuing its goals?

One solution, commonly adopted by capitalistic firms, is the hierarchical, vertical command system. Top management makes strategically important decisions that are transmitted downward, to be executed by those below. People inside the firm are divided into two categories: decision makers and decision followers. Each side has its own function to serve, and mixing the two functions will only jeopardize the efficiency of the system. The vertical command system is based on the principle of specialization. Each worker is a specialist concentrating on one job, and all jobs are carefully aligned to constitute a mechanism capable of implementing the decisions made at the top.

The hierarchical system is a rational and efficient modus operandi if demand for the firm's products is stable, products are homogenous or scarcely differentiated, and production involves only a few stages and relatively simple procedures. These conditions allow for a high degree of job specialization. With workers specializing and conforming to the vertical command, the firm should be able to efficiently mass-produce undifferentiated products.

The system, however, has its drawbacks. Since each worker is a specialist concerned only with his own job, intrafirm transfer of technical information and know-how is limited. The system requires many supervisors to oversee atomized workers, who are ill equipped to view the production process as a whole. The workers will not be able to solve local problems such as machine breakdown or equipment malfunction by themselves, and other specialists will be charged with fixing particular problems, which may be time consuming and costly. Inasmuch as workers are not expected to make contributions to managerial decisions, management may forgo much useful information of a sort that only those who are directly engaged in production can gather.

Perhaps the system's most serious problem is its inherent propensity to demoralize and alienate the workers. The system of vertical command, together with division of labor, depersonalizes the work environment. Once the workers pass through the company gates each morning, they are assumed to miraculously metamorphose themselves into beings without psychology, and to remain unaffected by the monotonous work routine. They are supposed to be machines with human faces, efficiently and emotionlessly performing specialized tasks. The uneducated and unsophisticated may be able to withstand the boredom of repeating the simple routine all day. As the level of education and literacy of workers rises, the same routine will increasingly become a source of tremendous frustration. The more self-esteem an individual possesses, the more he or she will expect out of the workday. Passive fulfullment of duties set by supervisors is demoralizing, and demoralization hinders productivity. The authoritarian command system is meant to maximize the firm's economic efficiency. Ironically, in the end, everyone may lose.

In contrast to the capitalistic firm, the humanistic firm commonly employs a decentralized decision making system. Management does not rigidly define and spell out the minute details of each job. Job categories are far fewer than in the capitalistic firm. Workers are expected and trained to be generalists. They regularly rotate jobs, learning multiple skills. They cultivate a habit of thinking holistically and a sense of coordination with other workers' performance. They are encouraged to define and improve their work standards. The multiple skills that they acquire include the ability to anticipate, diagnose, and solve local problems as they emerge, on their own. Most operational decision making is left to those on the shop floor, the assumption being that those closest to production know best about it. Enormous amounts of new information, ideas, and suggestions for quality improvement and productivity gains move from bottom up to management.

As a way to enable a large firm to behave like a well-motivated self-employed person, the humanistic firm is organized on the basis of small-group activity. One might not expect, out of a large number of disorganized individuals, high degrees of mutual communication and coordinated work effort. To counter this problem, the work force is divided into many small groups, each group (say, ten to fifteen workers) typically consisting of members of a shop. A group of ten people can easily get to know one another closely, even if ten thousand cannot, and communicate and cooperate among themselves effectively. Each group is left semiautonomous so that it can act coherently as a decentralized operational decision making unit. Yet it should not be too autonomous, since it must cooperate and coordinate with other groups so as to maximize the firm's overall productivity. To prevent each small group from becoming too autonomous, group leaders rotate supervising different groups at different times. A large task of management of the humanistic firm is to achieve a proper balance between autonomy and interdependence of small groups.

A small group might meet periodically to discuss all matters (large or small, technical or routine) so as to improve the quality, productivity, and safety of the work. The group may meet briefly the first thing in the morning to prepare for the day, or have a longer session in the afternoon after work on company time. The point of emphasis is continual improvement through incremental and systematic elimination of waste, irrationality, and irregularity from the jobs being performed.

The central objective of the system is to build a flexible and adaptable work force that can respond swiftly and smoothly to changing market conditions, to establish and maintain an organically integrated stock of human capital that can bend, twist, stretch, and expand itself as required for the firm's survival and growth. The system is peculiarly suited to the market environment, where demand frequently shifts, products to be produced are highly differentiated, and production involves many and complex stages and procedures.

The decentralized system, like any other system, has certain disadvantages. Thanks to an adaptive work force, local operational problems may be dealt with quickly. Strategic decisions, however, tend to take longer than under the vertical command system, as they are made consensually and with everyone's participation. The other side of the coin is that— given everyone's consensus and familiarity with the decision—once reached, it will be executed quickly and effectively.

Under the decentralized system the initial costs of training new workers are substantial. There is also an inherent danger that the emphasis on generalized (as against specialized) training will create a work force that consists of many a jack-of-all-trades and master of none. The assumption of the system is that in the long run these costs will be more than offset by the benefits of firmwide productivity gains derivable only from the slowly and carefully nurtured stock of human capital, free of the alienation associated with the authoritarian vertical command system.

The Incentive System

Shirking is generally not a problem for self-employed individuals. The picture changes, however, as we switch to a larger firm. Here the output is produced by a group of people rather than by one individual, tempting some to shirk in the name of their own self-interest. Shirking becomes a rational act when its benefit exceeds its cost. For example, if all workers on a production team are equally paid, shirking or no, and their employment is guaranteed, some of them will try to slack off at the expense of their fellows. If the shirking fever spreads to all members of the group, then output will decline precipitously. The firm goes bankrupt, and all the workers lose their jobs. Upon realizing that what may make sense to the individual will lead to collective collapse, the workers may spontaneously develop a peer-pressure system to discourage individual shirking.

Shirking is of little concern to the firm if the nature of production allows for a piece-rate system whereby each worker is paid on the basis of how much output he or she has actually produced (this is in effect the equivalent of a group of self-employed individuals working under the same roof). In the contemporary industrial economy, however, piece-rate systems are rare. A firm's overall output is produced in such a way that it is exceedingly difficult to measure how much any individual contributes; this setting provides fertile ground for shirking. The contemporary firm thus provides a setting that tempts, if not encourages, shirking.

One solution is to maintain sufficient supervisory personnel.

But it costs the firm to hire and train foremen to watch over workers, junior supervisors to oversee foremen, and senior supervisors to supervise junior supervisors. The supervisory approach is sensible only if increased productivity as a result of hiring supervisors outstrips the cost of employing them. In supervisory situations, workers play cat-and-mouse games, expending valuable time and energy on ingenious acts to conceal their shirking. The supervisory approach, if pushed too far, may turn out to be counterproductive. The most reliable kind of discipline is spontaneous, autonomously nurtured self-discipline. Implicit in the supervisory system is the assumption that workers cannot be trusted, and it is not unlikely that such an attitude will invite rebellion, becoming a self-fulfilling prophecy.

In the representative capitalistic firm, each worker, as a member of a production team, receives pay determined by a particular job rather than on the basis of how much the team produces. Of course, the more skilled the worker, the higher the pay; but there is no way to calculate whether or not one's pay exactly corresponds to one's contribution to the team's output. This system is bound to discourage cooperation among workers. Each worker is a specialist expected to perform one job, independently of the other workers. When worker A helps worker B, A's output will decrease and B's increase. The team's output will increase only if the former is smaller than the latter. Even if there is a net increase of the team's output, that will not immediately result in an upward adjustment of the pay scale. A hesitates to help B as he/she worries about management's negative evaluation of his/her work, while B may decide to shirk as a way of taking advantage of A's assistance, since B's greater output will not translate into higher pay.

In the context of the humanistic firm, on the other hand, the principle of sharing provides a powerful internal incentive system. Production is explicitly acknowledged as a matter of teamwork. Each worker is expected and encouraged to serve as a member of the team rather than on his or her own. The firm's ultimate goal is to maximize its output, and not the pro-

35

ductivity of a particular worker. Each individual worker's productivity is assessed in terms of its contribution to the firm's overall productivity. Thus the common criteria for evaluation of workers are: willingness to cooperate and coordinate with other workers; ability to assist, and be assisted by, others; eagerness to learn and accumulate multiple contextual skills; aptitude in solving problems and initiating new ideas useful for the firm; and aptitude for holistic thinking.

The humanistic firm's cooperative approach to production has a built-in tendency to discourage shirking. Workers are expected and trained to serve as members of a team rather than as specialists working independently of others. In the setting of explicitly group-oriented activity, noncooperation and shirking become easily detectable and highly visible. The other members exert tremendous pressure on one another, and will likely initiate a proposal that management dismiss those who, despite peer pressure, do not contribute their fair share. A related cost-saving advantage of the teamwork approach is that the firm needs to maintain fewer supervisors, since workers spontaneously develop self-discipline with a knowledge and understanding that they themselves will benefit.

An American auto worker at Nummi (a GM-Toyota joint venture in Fremont, California) was sent to Japan for special training, and was amazed at the high degree of teamwork among the Japanese Toyota workers. He reports: "When a worker got stuck with a problem, other members of his production team would immediately come to help him fix it. I never saw anything like that at the GM Fremont plant where I used to work. At GM you were on your own. If the next guy was having trouble, that was his business."

The process of promotion is slow, carefully designed, and multiphasic. Given the internalized labor market for the humanistic firm, people, as a rule, are recruited from within the firm for higher positions. Under the job-rotation system, each worker is evaluated by many different supervisors over a long period of time, a practice intended to minimize potential unfairness and subjective judgments. Workers have the right to bring their grievances to a higher supervisor, and to request a transfer to another section of the firm. Those supervisors who generate a large number of grievances definitely reduce their chances for further promotion.

The firm's attempt to build a flexible, adaptive, integrative work force starts early with new recruits. The firm is extraordinarily careful to hire high-performing graduates who have demonstrated a capacity for teamwork and an aptitude for working within a large, complex organization. The humanistic firm, like the capitalistic counterpart, is there to make money; it is not a re-education system for those who do not want to abide by its rules. Despite the care taken in initial screening, mistakes inevitably are made. The internalized labor market does not necessitate a worker's permanent employment-agreement problem. The firm does fire incompetent workers or those who demonstrate unethical behavior.

The recruited workers begin a long journey to become integral elements of the firm. As time goes by, they are slowly divided into two broad categories: those who are notably self-motivating, cooperative, flexible, adaptable; and those who are not. The former are candidates for higher positions, and the latter are understood to be off the promotional ladder. Those in the second group may not be up for promotion, but they are considered to be sufficiently competent to serve as members of the firm.

How does the firm sustain the overall morale of its work force, especially of the latter group? First, the system of slow and multiphasic promotion minimizes the demoralizing effect on the group as a whole of favoritism or jump promotion. It allows for slow starters and gives workers second and third chances. The prime intent of the system is that when particular individuals are finally promoted, there is a wide consensus among their colleagues that they are the natural, logical choices.

Second, the compensation system is adjusted to maintain high overall morale of the work force. Total pay includes merit pay and seniority pay. Merit pay is to recognize and reward those with exceptional talent and ability. Seniority pay compensates all workers, including the less talented and less capable, for their long-term contributions to the firm. The system is based on the principle of what might be called "competitive egalitarianism"—that is, the winners and losers are both members of the same enterprise, and therefore those who win should not be excessively rewarded and those who lose should not be exceedingly penalized.

The principle of competitive egalitarianism also emphasizes a fair distribution of "total" compensation consisting of pecuniary as well as psychic rewards. The young and extraordinarily talented are often given important and responsible assignments, which give them psychic income (satisfaction), offsetting the relatively small pecuniary income that comes with their low seniority. The humanistic scheme of compensation does have an inherent disadvantage in that it will not attract those who are highly talented but feel incurably uncomfortable with the ethos of egalitarianism, or those single-mindedly interested in maximization of their pecuniary income.

Management

In contemporary America, managers are professionalized and recruited from the external market. Largely because of their professionalization, top executives command enormous salaries (to say nothing of bonuses and other benefits), and maintain a life-style—in terms of office amenities, housing, transportation, vacationing, entertainment, recreation—distinct from that of other employees of the same firm. They form a pecuniary "aristocracy" of America, a peculiar anomaly for a nation that, since its founding, has vigorously upheld and practiced democracy in politics.

Conventional economics of the neoclassical variety offers a simple explanation for this, usually described as "the marginal-productivity theory of wage." When the firm hires more and more workers, its total revenue increases at a diminishing rate, reflecting the lowered marginal productivity of labor as more labor is combined with the fixed stock of capital in the firm. Given the prevailing wage, the firm will continue to hire additional labor until the marginal revenue product of labor per hour (i.e., an increase in total revenue resulting from hiring additional labor per person-hour worked) becomes equal to the prevailing hourly wage. In other words, how much one is paid by the firm is indicative of the dollar's worth of one's marginal productivity.

The theory says in effect that two workers, A and B, earn $40,000 and $20,000, respectively, because A is twice as productive as B. Such a proposition may be construed as an apologia for the status quo or a meaningless exercise in tautology.

Applied to a chief executive earning an annual salary of a million dollars, the theory suggests that his presence is enhancing the firm's total revenue by at least $1 million per annum, and his absence will reduce total revenue by $1 million or more. By the same logic, then, if total revenue decreases by $100 million during his tenure, it means that his true marginal revenue product is minus $100 million and therefore he owes the firm $100 million plus the salary he has received. It is improbable that, when fired, he will repay his debt. On the contrary, he will likely walk away with a golden parachute containing generous severance pay and other benefits as stipulated by his contract. It is often held that an enormous salary is a necessary incentive for executives charged with hard and demanding tasks. The fact is, top executives of American capitalism are members of an extraordinarily privileged class, richly rewarded for their successes *and* failures: their existence makes a mockery of the self-disciplinary market.

In the context of the humanistic enterprise system, management assumes a different kind of role. Most managers at all levels are recruited internally. They are not professionalized, and their salaries are modest by American standards. But along with their pecuniary incomes, managers of the humanistic firm earn considerable amounts of psychic income in intrafirm and social respect and prestige.

At each level, new managers are selected by both their superiors and their subordinates; candidates highly regarded by superiors but disrespected by those below have little chance of promotion. Managers are chosen on the basis of their demonstrated leadership quality in promoting and sustaining the cooperative and integrative work efforts of all workers, in building consensus for projects large and small, and in coordinating activities under their jurisdiction with those elsewhere in the firm. Because of the slow and multistage promotion process, usually few in the firm are surprised when the next top and senior executives are introduced.

Management of the humanistic firm works in an environment essentially free of the ideological constraints of capitalism. There is no group external to the firm that may threaten the integrity and autonomy of management. There is no pressure from anyone on management to struggle constantly to maximize the firm's short-run profits; the firm's central objective is long-term prosperity and growth. Management represents the interest of the firm, which coincides with that of all who work within it.

From a capitalistic perspective, such an environment might appear to breed laxity and complacency: no stockholders look over management's shoulders; workers are friendly and cooperative; there is no relentless pressure for quick profit maximization. If mismanagement occurs, who will enact discipline? Although the question is logical in the context of capitalism, it does not really apply to the humanistic firm. Management of the humanistic firm is hardly free of all disciplinary constraints. As described above, one source of discipline is internal and self-imposed: all within the firm stand to gain or lose depending on the firm's performance. In addition, workers can guard against management's malperformance and possible abuse of its power by expressing their collective voice through their enterprise union. When mismanagement does occur, the problem is dealt with internally—those responsible are replaced by the next executives in line or other senior managers who are better suited for solving particular problems.

This way, workers are free at least of anxiety occasioned by outside takeovers or imposed management replacements who may turn out to be even worse.

Another source of discipline, market competition, is external. What is prone to induce management's complacency is the firm's monopolistic position, rather than the conspicuous absence of an external group overseeing management's behavior. The humanistic firm is an independent, autonomous entity, but this does not make it monopolistic. On the contrary, the firm operates in fierce competition with other firms. Management of the humanistic firm is compelled to discipline itself with the knowledge that the price of losing competition through complacency will be exceedingly high. Generally speaking, then, workers in the capitalistic firm are disciplined by management, which in turn is disciplined by capitalists who enjoy, more or less, a free reign with no one to discipline them. In the humanistic firm, both management and workers are systemically led to spontaneously discipline themselves.

Enterprise Union

In classical capitalism, the union, as an institution of collective bargaining between labor and management, does not exist. In a world of minifirms employing only a handful of workers, there is little rationale for organizing labor to confront management. Typically, unskilled and easily replaceable workers receive market wages, and are at the mercy of the capitalist-owner of the firm where they work. If they are dissatisfied, they may engage in passive resistance by shirking as much as possible, only to be fired before long, or they voluntarily quit the firm in search of a more merciful employer.

Under contemporary capitalism, with the coming of large corporations, the power relation between labor and management begins to change. The representative firm operating in a certain industry (steel, automobiles, etc.) employs a mixture of skilled, semiskilled, and unskilled workers, and management becomes increasingly dependent on labor. Management, however, does not represent the interests of labor, and therefore workers must protect their own interests. One way is individual bargaining, a worker presenting his/her grievances to management in the hope that the individual employee's voice will be duly heard. Collective bargaining is another, usually more effective way, wherein a common interest is promoted through a united front. The emergence of an industrial (or craft) union thus is a predictable and logical development in the context of contemporary capitalism.

Under the humanistic enterprise system, where management and workers already share a common interest and common identity, the idea of an industrial union makes little sense. Each humanistic firm is a free, independent, and autonomous unit of production competing with other humanistic firms. To workers in one firm, workers in other firms are rivals, if not enemies, threatening their survival. The environment is structured so that competition is "firm versus firm" rather than "labor versus management." Still, if the humanistic firm consists of many workers, there are practical reasons for the existence of some kind of union.

In contemporary Japan the predominant form of labor organization is the enterprise union (not to be confused with "company" union, relatively popular in the United States in the 1920s, sponsored by, and under the paternalistic influence of, management). The enterprise union consists of all workers in the firm, from production to administrative. All workers being managers of sorts under the decentralized decision-making system, there is no clear line of demarcation between management and workers. There is a continuity between management and the union membership. Managers at all levels are normally selected from among the unionized workers (not recruited from outside the firm), and a fair number of senior executives (about seventeen percent) are former union officials who were promoted to executive positions for their abilities in the areas of interpersonal networking, administration, arbitration, and conflict resolution and leadership. In consequence, one peculiar problem in organizing the enterprise union is to determine who are managers and therefore should not be members of the union.

The union contract with capitalistic management in America tends to be complete, explicit, narrowly focused, and long-term. The contract is in effect a manifesto of mutual distrust between labor and management, with both sides insisting on complete exposition of what is negotiated and exact and explicit wording of every clause. Once signed into effect, the contract is not renewable for two to three years. Given the sharp functional distinction between management and labor, the decisions that will affect the future of the firm are within the jurisdiction of management and are not subject to collective bargaining.

In contrast, the enterprise union in the humanistic firm exists not to confront management, but as a medium for both workers and management to share information and decision making on all important matters. The union acts primarily as an institutionalized channel of intrafirm communication.

Union and management discuss and negotiate a wide range of issues: wages and salaries, bonuses, fringe benefits, work standards, seniority rights, hiring and layoff policy, in-house training schedules, personnel transfers, relocation of factories, R and D plans, and so on. Management routinely shares with the union financial information of the sort that would be deemed proprietary in the American context, and discusses major managerial decisions, both strategic and operational, in order to achieve mutual understanding and agreement. Close attention is always paid to the proper balancing of benefits and costs, prerogatives and obligations, among all ranks and parties involved.

Since the benefits and costs of being members of the same firm are substantially shared, workers are firmly aware that the fruits of their extra efforts will not be appropriated by someone else; such awareness serves as a powerful source of spontaneous self-motivation. Consequently, the contract between the enterprise union and management tends to be general and implicit rather than specific and explicit. This implicit contract gives management the advantage of being able to flexibly readjust work schedules as dictated by changing business conditions. In addition, wages and salaries are negotiated and settled annually, and bonuses semiannually. Sequential bargaining over compensation makes labor cost variable instead of fixed, providing management considerable leeway to maneuver through hard times.

The same leeway is often not available to management of the capitalistic firm, constrained as it is by explicit, long-term contracts that minutely detail work rules and compensations. From the union's perspective, the explicit contract is needed to avoid exploitation. For management, such an explicit contract is also necessary because without it workers, knowing that the fruits of their extra work effort will not likely be theirs, would rationally be inclined to minimize their effort expenditures. The managerial inflexibility imposed by the explicit contract and labor's lack of self-motivation adversely affect the firm's productivity. For its part, the fixity of wages means that when demand for the firm's products starts to fall in recession, management cannot lower prices to sustain the level of output because unit labor cost cannot be reduced accordingly. The firm is therefore compelled to adjust to the weakening demand by curtailing production and laying off redundant workers.

When an American friend of mine heard about the enterprise union in Japan, he said, "Seems utopian." However, the enterprise union as described above operates at almost all corporations practicing human capitalism in Japan today. But, it is not a pie that suddenly dropped from the sky. We will see in Chapter 4 that during the early postwar years, management-labor relations in Japan were often confrontational and sometimes even bloody. The enterprise union is a new institution that management and workers created together after many arduous years of trial and error.

Patterns of Competition

The theory of capitalism is founded on the idea that competition is what promotes and sustains the efficiency and dynamism of the economic system. In Adam Smith's famous metaphor, market competition is the "invisible hand" that transforms the sellers' private greed for profits into social good.

Under capitalism, both in theory and practice, competition takes place, as a rule, between individuals. Workers compete for better jobs as individuals. Managers strive for higher positions on their own. Individual entrepreneurs compete with other individual entrepreneurs. One is left with an impression that true competition is a human activity that can occur only between individuals—which obviously is untrue. Even in America, where the individualistic ideology remains strong, many people participate in group as well as individual sports. Competition between baseball teams can be as fierce as that between two lone golfers.

In the context of the humanistic enterprise system, competition tends to be primarily group oriented. Workers within each firm compete with one another for promotion; however, they cooperate with each other toward maximizing the competitive power of their firm against other firms. Most humanistic firms belong to an enterprise group. The firms belonging to the same group assist one another in varied ways, whereas vigorous competition persists between different enterprise groups.

The industrial development and growth of the capitalistic countries in the West during the nineteenth and twentieth centuries provide powerful circumstantial evidence that individual-oriented competition is a viable form of competition to promote the dynamism of the market economy. Likewise, Japan's postwar economic successes, happening within the framework of intergroup competition, strongly suggest that group-oriented competition also can be a highly effective framework of Adam Smith's "invisible hand." Conventional neoclassical economics makes the assumption that competition is necessarily individual oriented, and that competition and cooperation belong to two distinctly separate categories of human activity. This is peculiar because even in the West, group-oriented competition is not uncommon in athletic, political, social, military, and other activities.

3

BETWEEN MARKET
AND ORGANIZATION

❏

Organized Market

Conventional economics perceives market and organization as two distinct modes of economic transactions. The market is where individual buyers and sellers freely make their own independent decisions in pursuit of self-interest as they interact with one another. A buyer and a seller each represent a different interest; the former seeks the lowest price, while the latter tries to charge as high a price as possible. The fundamental market principle therefore is competition. It makes little sense for those with conflicting interests to help each other.

For a variety of reasons initially free and independent individuals may decide to organize themselves into a group with a common cause. As they become parts of an organization, they are expected to comply with the basic organization rule: cooperation. The firm is a representative form of economic organization. Those inside it are free to exit as they wish, but as long as they stay with the firm, they are obliged to engage in cooperative and collaborative work efforts consistent with the firm's objective.

Both market and organization have inherent advantages and disadvantages. Those who operate in the market are free and independent agents; hence they are likely to be highly motivated. Free from organizational constraints, they have wide access to information available from anyone in the market. At the same time they are strangers competing against each other, and therefore accumulation of mutually beneficial knowledge and know-how among them will be limited. Further, as they deal in the market, where everything is settled on the spot, their outlook will tend to be shortsighted.

In contrast, those who work within an organized framework are likely to be able to store and develop mutually useful information. Since members of an organization are in a joint long-term venture, they are apt to have a farsighted or long-run perspective on their activity. On the other hand, they may be less motivated, inasmuch as they work for the group rather than for themselves. Interacting only with a limited number of people within the same organization, they will suffer from a limited access to information, relative to those operating in a free, open market.

Which of the two—market or organization—is a more efficient way of producing output largely depends on circumstances. In the textbook world of perfect competition, where a large number of atomized sellers compete in selling one simple, homogeneous product to numerous buyers, and market information is readily available, it is doubtful that organizing agents into a group will bring about any visible benefits. Anyone in need of the product can easily get it anytime on the spot at its lowest possible price. Such a world, however, rarely exists in reality.

We live in the world of oligopoly and monopolistic competition, where most products are highly differentiated and embody complex technology. The market we face is often segmented into blocs of buyers preferring nonstandard goods, instead of numerous buyers seeking a homogeneous product. In such a world how to reduce the transaction cost becomes a significant issue.

Under perfect competition transaction cost is negligible. Many sellers are selling the identical product at the same lowest price. All you have to do is to buy one from any seller, and the transaction is complete. Buying it from another seller will make no difference. The same is not true if the products you desire are differentiated in price, quality, design, replaceability, maintenance requirement, and the like.

In order to purchase one of these differentiated products in the market, you must begin gathering all information on it for careful analysis and assessment. After scaling available alternatives down to a few that are best in your judgment, you proceed to contact prospective sellers of the product. Following correspondence and telephone calls come meetings with salespeople. If the product is expensive, you might prudently ask an attorney to draft an elaborate contract to minimize your potential loss. The seller's attorney objects to the wording of clauses here and there. The two attorneys may need to get together several times to resolve their differences.

Once the contract is finally signed, you are still not certain the product will be delivered undamaged on time, or if it will really function as claimed by the seller. In the event that it turns out to be defective, will it be quickly replaced with a new one as stipulated by the contract? What about unforeseeable and uncontrollable circumstances that will make it impossible for you or the seller to honor the contractual obligations? Thus the transaction cost associated with your attempt to purchase the product from the external market keeps piling up.

One way to eliminate the transaction cost incurred by dependence on the market is to internalize the market, i.e., let your firm produce the needed product for and by itself. An automobile manufacturing company can produce steel, parts, and components that it needs instead of purchasing them from the external suppliers. This approach may solve one problem, but it creates others: employees who produce the product for the firm, rather than for themselves, may not be as motivated as the free agents operating in the open market; the producers inside the firm have less access to technical as well as practical information relative to those in the external market, and such information shortage will adversely affect the innovativeness of the internalized producers and the quality of their product. Moreover, the in-house production facilities, once built, become a large fixed-cost element for the firm that cannot easily be eliminated should market conditions subsequently change, reducing demand for internal production.

In reality, market and organization often are not separated

from one another in sharp dichotomy. Rather, between the two is a wide middle zone or an intermediate market where market principles and organization principles, to varying degrees, are blended together. Economic agents compete or cooperate with one another, depending on circumstances. Let us call this middle zone the "organized market."

To illustrate, suppose the firm develops a long-term business relationship with three independent suppliers. People in the firm and the suppliers get well acquainted thanks to their steady, long-term mutual dealings. In consequence, they can communicate faster and more effectively. Each is thoroughly aware of the other's particular problems, strengths, and weaknesses. They often cooperate in order to solve their problems jointly. The firm may make suggestions to the suppliers for quality improvements, or the suppliers convey innovative ideas to the firm for consideration.

The long-term collaborative relationship does not mean, however, that the suppliers have been internalized by and for the firm. They are independent agents who may deal with other firms, and at the same time the firm provides no assurance that the relationship is exclusive and permanent. There is always a subtle hint that if Supplier A's performance is not satisfactory, the firm may terminate its ties with A and shift the deals to B, C, or any other suppliers.

The organized market may be construed as an attempt to integrate the advantage of human networking into the market rule of competition, an attempt to make competition and cooperation complementary rather than substitutional. It is a way simultaneously to combine and preserve the merits of market and organization and eliminate their demerits, to make economic agents motivated, well-informed, farsighted, and willing to accumulate mutually beneficial knowledge. There is no automatic assurance, however, that the organized market always achieves such an ideal. Conceivably it can degenerate in the worst possible way, losing the merits of competition and cooperation while combining the defects of market and organization: shortsightedness, unwillingness to accumulate mutually useful knowledge, lack of motivation, and information shortage.

The humanistic firm, more than its capitalistic counterpart, tends to rely on the organized market in dealing, not only with goods, but also with personnel and financial capital. Thus when the firm faces a dire need to relocate personnel beyond itself, say, because of a depression or a major shift in the industrial structure, it commonly depends, for their absorption, on the extensive network of firms belonging to the same enterprise group (see page 53). The ability, talent, aptitude, and experiences of people to be transferred are carefully examined and compared in terms of specific needs and expectations on the part of the receiving firms so that, when they arrive, there will be no disappointments or unpleasant surprises.

In the area of finance the representative humanistic firm usually develops and maintains a close, long-term, collaborative relationship with a major bank or two within the same enterprise group in order to enhance, as it were, the efficiency of money. The bank often assigns its personnel, on a visiting basis, to the borrowing firm to get better acquainted with the firm's financial conditions and requirements so that the bank's lending policy may be sound and correct. Money does not change hands mechanically and impersonally through the open money market. Instead it moves via a dense human network based on mutual knowledge, information, and trust.

Large manufacturing firms in Japan extensively practice subcontracting as a means of avoiding the diseconomies of scale (problems that arise when a company gets too big) and of developing the strategic flexibility of the firm by taking full advantage of the organized market. The major manufacturing firm commonly establishes a long-term business relationship (renewable every four or five years) with several (rather than many) competing subcontracting firms for supplies of parts, components, and equipment. Each of these subcontracting firms, in turn, deals with several major manufacturing firms in lieu of establishing an exclusive relationship with any one of them. The manufacturer's selection of its subcontractors is deliberate, cautious, and measured; it invests an extraordinary amount of resources in investigating the quality, reliability, and innovativeness of subcontracting work from a long-range perspective before entering into a new relationship with a particular subcontracting firm.

Subcontractors are often partially owned by the manufacturing firm, but essentially they are separate, independent entities rather than internal components of the latter. They have the liberty of not renewing the current contract and of turning to establish a new relationship with another manufacturer. At the same time the manufacturing firm is under no obligation to perpetuate the present ties with the select subcontractors. The manufacturing firm fiercely competes with other manufacturing firms in the finished-goods market while keen competition prevails among subcontractors. In other words, the major manufacturing firm and its affiliated subcontractors are semi-integrated on the basis of a semipermanent, cooperative relationship.

How the fruits of the cooperative efforts are shared between the major manufacturing firm and a subcontracting firm largely depends on the nature of the product the latter is able to supply. If the subcontractor holds a relatively monopolistic position on its particular product, its bargaining power with the manufacturing firm will be correspondingly high, and it can command an equitable share of the fruit. On the other hand, the bargaining power of the subcontracting firm supplying only standard, easily replaceable products is weak, and workers in such a firm are known to receive lower wages than do those at the subcontracting firms supplying advanced parts and components.

This extensive reliance on coalitional subcontracting should be construed as a case of extending the system of decentralized decision making beyond the firm. The underlying logic and rationale are the same. The manufacturer does not unilaterally tell the subcontractor what to supply. The manufacturer is aware that those who actually produce parts and components possess intimate and technical knowledge of the sort not easily acquirable at the manufacturer's level. The subcontractor, similarly, realizes that those who assemble finished goods face particular problems concerning parts and components that cannot be readily perceived at the subcontractor's level. Hence decision making is shared and kept substantially decentralized with a constant two-way flow of information, ideas, and suggestions for quality control and solution of technical problems. Such a flow has the added value of motivating all parties concerned.

Enterprise Groups

We have seen that the representative humanistic firm is a large manufacturing concern whose work force is substantially internalized, where management and workers constitute an almost completely integrated group sharing a common goal, and that maintains a close network of semiintegrated subcontracting relations with smaller firms in the context of an organized market. Another aspect of the humanistic enterprise system as it operates in contemporary Japan is that the firms form, and belong to, wider circles of corporate grouping—which we shall call "enterprise groups."

A representative enterprise group consists of a major city bank, a major trading company, and a major manufacturing firm as the central core of the group, and of several large manufacturing firms in different product lines, below which lie pyramids of affiliated smaller subcontracting firms. It is impossible to determine who ultimately owns and controls the group because the core firms (and, to a smaller extent, lesser member firms) practice extensive, multidirectional mutual stockholding. The major bank holds stock in the trading company and the manufacturing firms, and vice versa; at the same time the bank's stock is substantially owned by the nation's prime insurance companies, which are typically mutual cooperatives rather than joint stock companies (Tables VI and VII in Appendix).

Each enterprise group is a loose network of coalitional re-

lations among the firms. There is no charter, code, or constitution that carefully and precisely spells out rights and
obligations of the member firms. Each enterprise group has a
Presidents' Club whose members—chief executive officers of
the major firms within the group—periodically meet and informally exchange information and ideas; but the club makes no
highest-level, groupwide managerial decisions. We cannot
even describe each group as a clearly cohesive entity. Its membership is variable and fluid over time rather than constant and
permanent. The trading company does not exclusively deal
with member firms; some of its clients may be firms affiliated
with other enterprise groups. Though the bank extends its
credit mainly to member firms, its loans are available to worthy customers outside the group. There is nothing fixed about
affiliation between the prime manufacturing firm and its
subcontractors.

Each enterprise group may be understood as a set of overlapping organized markets in which the member firms form
long-lasting cooperative relations on many levels. The goal of
corporate grouping is to reduce transaction costs and to enhance joint productivity through collaborative work efforts. By
maintaining a long-term, mutually supportive relationship
people in two firms get better acquainted with each other's
needs and difficulties, and hence become able to communicate
and solve problems faster and more effectively. The bank provides credit to the affiliated trading company with full knowledge of its internal conditions and policy directions. The
trading company in turn selectively extends credit to the affiliated firms with prudence based on a thorough familiarity with
each firm's particular projects and related financial requirements. The manufacturing firm relies on the trading company
for distribution and marketing of its products so as to derive
benefits from the latter's experience and expertise.

Interfirm deals are negotiated from the perspective of long-
term mutual assistance and coprosperity. Yet in order to avoid
complacency and sluggishness that may stem from rigid orga-

nization of resources, the affiliated firms are only semiintegrated, and on a nonpermanent basis. There is a constant and subtle mutual reminder that the coalitional relation is to continue only as long as it produces visible and significant mutual benefits. Otherwise, it may at any time be terminated.

It is known that the enterprise-group-affiliated firms on the whole produce somewhat lower but more stable profits, and workers therein earn higher wages, in comparison with nonaffiliated firms. The fact that workers at the affiliated firms receive higher wages is no surprise, since a main objective of enterprise grouping is, through application of the principles of organized market, to maximize joint productivity, the fruits of which are to be shared among all parties concerned. The pattern of lower but more stable profits among the affiliated firms suggests that their interest is not in short-term profit-maximization but in long-term survival, growth, and coprosperity. In other words, each enterprise group in effect functions as a scheme of risk diversification or as a security insurance arrangement for mutual protection.

In the United States employer/employee contributions to retirement benefits are commonly invested in a diversified portfolio of securities at a pension fund, external to the firm, and there are legal limits to the fund's investing in the stock of one company. Under this legal system of risk diversification the employees of the representative American firm enjoy the security of their retirement benefits and a reasonable degree of assurance that they can recover their benefits in the dire event of the firm's bankruptcy. In contrast, in contemporary Japan the pension reserve is typically invested in the firm's own assets, and therefore the internalized workers at the representative firm assume a high risk, if their firm fails, of losing their premium wages as well as severance pay. Formation of an enterprise group may be construed as a way of diversifying such risks.

Affiliated firms implicitly agree to offer mutual assistance in difficult times. When a firm starts to experience a serious financial crisis, rescue usually comes not from the state but from the affiliated firms. The banks pool their resources to provide an emergency credit line. The affiliated manufacturing firms and/or the trading company supply their expert personnel to the firm in trouble, for technical aid and consultancy. Once the crisis is over, the saved firm is expected to repay its debts to the rescuers in future years.

Nissan's 1990 "takeover" of Fuji Heavy Industries, the maker of Subaru automobiles, illustrates the discreet manner in which a company rescue is commonly administered within the framework of an enterprise group. After a period of declining sales of Subaru cars in the United States and Japan, Fuji registered an operating loss of $200 million in 1989. With Fuji's financial position critically weakening, Nissan (the country's number-two auto giant, holding a long-term cooperative alliance with Fuji), the Industrial Bank (Fuji's main creditor), and the company in trouble began intensive negotiations to deal with the situation. According to the agreement reached in July 1990, Nissan will effectively take over Fuji by appointing its senior executive as Fuji's new president, replacing the old president, who will assume the ceremonial position of chairman—with an understanding that production of Subaru cars will continue, though on a smaller scale, and Nissan, now stretched to capacity, will convert Fuji's excess facilities into secondary plants to produce Nissan models. Unlike a familiar scene in America, there will be no purge of executives or mass layoff of auto workers at Fuji, everyone will save face, and not a share of stock will change hands.

Since application of the principles of organization will yield fruit only if sufficiently exposed to the forces of competition, the viability of an enterprise group presupposes the presence of market competition. If only one enterprise group exists, it will probably become a de facto monopoly with all the adverse effects on the nation's economic welfare. The affiliated firms will direct their cooperative efforts toward maximization of monopoly profits at the expense of consumers. In contemporary Japan, however, such is hardly the case. There are six major enterprise groups, each operating in all major industries simultaneously. As a result there is fierce competition between and among the enterprise groups. Even within a group, competition persists among subcontractors and between the firms in similar product lines. Further, all enterprise groups constantly face keen competition from independent firms, including former affiliates, whose management tends to be more entrepreneurial and less risk averse than that of the affiliated firm.

As in the United States contemporary Japan has antitrust laws. An attempt by one major enterprise group to merge with another in order to form a new, supersize enterprise group will predictably invite a stern sanction from the Fair Trade Commission. To date there has been no such an attempt, nor will there likely be in the future. In reality, an enterprise group is a flexible coalition of semiintegrated firms whose membership and direction are in a state of constant flux. Each enterprise group is already huge in terms of the number of firms and people involved. Even setting aside antitrust sanctions a supersize enterprise group would suffer from tremendous organizational diseconomies of scale. The costs of organization would exceed its benefits, hindering the group's joint productivity. Only efficiency sustains each group's long-term viability in both the domestic and overseas markets. A megamerger would threaten the very survival of all groups concerned.

Enterprise groups may be perceived as a prototype of the humanistic enterprise system but not as an inevitable or necessary component of human capitalism. Traditional capitalism has produced somewhat different modes of private enterprise systems, such as corporatism in Western Europe, whereby big business, organized labor, and the state constitute a triad of countervailing forces, and state-guided capitalism in South Korea, Taiwan, and Singapore. When transplanted to other countries, human capitalism may or may not nurture the growth of enterprise groups of the sort found in contemporary Japan. To date there are no institutions comparable to them in the United States.

Innovations

The continual flow of technological innovations is what sustains the growth of the firms and of the nation's economy. What sort of an environment is most conducive to the blossoming of innovative thinking? The dynamic industrial growth of the free-enterprise economies in the West during the nineteenth century indicates that the freedom of individuals is a vital factor. In the age of classical capitalism individuals were free to think and create on their own. Original and daring innovations enabled them to win competition in the marketplace, and they were the ones to collect the rich harvest.

What is true for an individual should also be true for the firm. An innovative firm is likely one that is free to think and decide on its own. In the contemporary industrial world the firm should be as autonomous as possible from the standpoint of encouraging its innovative activity. This condition is not met under socialism, where management of the firm is controlled by the state. But it is not fully met under capitalism either. Management of the capitalistic firm is constrained by the propensity of the institutional investors or major individual capitalists to intervene in management decisions (they may, for example, opt for higher dividends and object to a proposed increase in R and D expenditures). The same management also faces another interventionist force, the union, which, concerned with job security of its members, may oppose management's attempt to introduce a new automation technology.

Compared with socialistic and capitalistic firms the humanistic firm enjoys the highest degree of freedom from restrictive outside influences. It is completely free of state intervention, and almost completely free of capitalist interference. The enterprise union is an integral component of the firm, sharing a common interest with management. The autonomy and freedom of the humanistic firm may therefore be held largely responsible for the impressive inventiveness demonstrated by Japanese firms in such areas as telecommunication, industrial ceramics, automobiles, television, VCR, robotics, electromechanics, and semiconductors.

The number of U.S. patents granted to American inventors peaked in 1972, and has been decreasing since. The share of U.S. patents held by U.S. residents dropped from eighty percent in 1965 to fifty-five percent in 1986 while, during the same period, the share of U.S. patents granted to foreign investors increased, with two thirds of the increase awarded to the Japanese nationals.

In 1977 the United States held the unchallenged technological lead in the semiconductor industry. The Defense Science Policy Board reports, however, that the Japanese firms today maintain the leadership position in a range of critical areas of the industry, and the range is quickly widening. Similar trends have also been observed in the computer and telecommunications industries.

A comparative study of flexible manufacturing systems (FMS) by Jay Jakimar (*Harvard Business Review,* November–December 1986) found that the number of parts made by an FMS is almost ten times greater, and the rate of new-product introduction per FMS is twenty-two times faster, in Japan than in America.

According to a study by the National Science Foundation, in 1988 Japan was not only ahead of the United States but also gaining ground in the following areas: *(in basic research)* fiber optics, integrated circuits, and mobile radio systems; *(in advanced development)* automated factory assembly, compact-disk technology, fiber optics, and integrated circuits; *(in product manufacturing/engineering)* automated factory assembly, compact-disk technology, computer design, computer software, fiber optics, and integrated circuits.

The humanistic firm embodies certain constitutional properties that inherently encourage innovation. The enterprise union supports and actively participates in the firm's innovative efforts; its members know that if the firm's technology stands still, it is only a matter of time before the firm will start to slip behind. Under the job-security rule the workers all understand that introduction of new technology is to enhance the firm's productivity and competitiveness and not to replace labor. To oppose it is like cutting one's own throat. The enterprise union will fully endorse it for the sake of its own survival.

The humanistic firm internalizes its workers and heavily invests in their in-house training in order to build a formidable stock of human capital capable of adding extra value to the firm's output. Under the minimum-layoff policy these workers, once internalized, cannot easily be dismissed. At the same time the firm is under constant pressure to keep on growing so as not to lose its market share to competing firms. The firm can increase its output by hiring more labor or by adopting a more capital/technology-intensive mode of production. The internalized labor market and the pressure for continual growth thus provide a built-in tendency for the humanistic firm to choose the capital/technology-intensive approach to achieve its growth objective. The firm welcomes and encourages technological innovations as a matter of necessity for its long-term survival, and the resultant productivity gains sustain the firm's competitiveness and allow for higher wages of the internalized workers.

According to the conventional textbook model the process of innovation moves in linear fashion from scientific research to product development to production of the product and to marketing. In reality, however, this is merely one scenario among many. Sometimes a new idea is first discovered on the shop floor and then is conveyed to a research engineer. Inspired and stimulated by the idea, the engineer proceeds to design a new product of a sort that he or she might not have developed alone. Similarly, there may be frequent and intensive exchange of information between the shop floor and the engineering department before an innovation is brought to fruition.

In the representative American firm, product development and the solution of technical problems are the engineers' responsibility and no concern of production workers. In the humanistic firm, on the other hand, operational decision making is largely decentralized, and the shopworkers are expected not only to solve local problems on their own but also, together with engineers, to produce innovative results. In fact, many of the innovative ideas actually adopted originally come from the shop floor.

In particular, progress in high technology (e.g., optics, bio-technology, electronics, new metals, information processing) requires constant and intense cross-fertilization of ideas among different industries. In light of this enterprise groups offer the advantage of flexible adaptability to the needs of the new era. An enterprise group is not industry based. Rather, it includes many firms, large and small, operating in different industries, and these firms are semi-integrated by a network of technical information and personnel. The human and technical network-ing across industries, as allowed by enterprise groups, is bound to facilitate cross-germination of ideas and interindustry R and D.

Inherent Problems

The humanistic firm emphasizes the principle of internal har-mony and cooperation in order to develop a highly integrated set of workers jointly striving toward maximization of the firm's output. What this means in practice is that the same people work together, face to face, within the same firm over a long period of time. Such an environment gives the impres-sion, especially to those with a capitalistic mind-set, of a house ideally suited for nurturing a closed, exclusionistic men-tality among its members.

It may be argued a priori that since the theme of the house is harmony and cooperation, nobody wishes to shake the apple-cart and everybody passively conforms to the group's rules and expectations. Great talents, mavericks, big thinkers, those who think the unthinkable, are despised and ostracized. Find-ing the place suffocatingly dull and inflexible, the free and original minds either do not join the house or leave it shortly after joining. The house will become a haven for a bunch of ordinary, small thinkers.

That the humanistic firm fosters a tendency toward complacency and sluggishness is a possibility. At the same time we should keep two things in mind. First, the internalized workforce is exposed to two elements of competition: intrafirm competition for promotion to higher positions; and keen interfirm competition for market shares. Second, truly original, creative thinkers are rare. Most of us are ordinary beings, neither geniuses nor morons, with varying degrees of potentially realizable creativity. The humanistic firm is meant to be of, for, and by the ordinary majority, and aims at mobilizing small creativities for generation of a whole that is greater than the sum of its parts. Nothing prevents the humanistic firm from embracing true talents, provided that they feel comfortable with the ethos of competitive egalitarianism and can remain active within such a work environment. If not, they would spontaneously and necessarily start their own ventures to privatize the fruit of their rare creativity.

The humanistic firm deals with its internal problems consensually and with everyone's participation. Anything is changeable and adjustable for the good of the firm with the agreement and understanding of its members. Suppose the existing egalitarian wage scale proves increasingly inadequate as shown by difficulties in recruiting or retaining truly talented workers, and there is clear evidence that the insufficiency of pecuniary rewards is the primary cause of the trouble. In this situation the firm has a choice between doing nothing about the problem or taking corrective measures, such as making the wage scale less egalitarian, with extra rewards for special talents. Adoption of a new wage scale, meant for betterment of the firm's performance, should not demoralize the work force if it is based on a wide consensus among the workers. Similarly, the firm may consensually modify its seniority rule to allow younger talents with less seniority to assume important positions, without violating the principles of humanistic enterprise.

Conventional wisdom holds that radical, revolutionary ideas are more likely to come from free-spirited, independent entrepreneurs than from the guardians of the well-established corporate regimes. Japan's postwar experience suggests, however, that the humanistic corporate regime does not necessarily imply the waning of entrepreneurship and is perfectly capable of absorbing great innovative talents. Akio Morita, Soichiro Honda, and Konosuke Matsushita are such examples. Morita, an unemployed navy engineer at the end of World War II, co-founded Sony Corporation with the initial paid-in capital of five hundred dollars. Honda and Matsushita, men of little formal education, founded Honda Motors and Matsushita Electric, respectively. These firms began as small, obscure concerns owned and controlled by their founders. They have grown to become multibillion-dollar global corporations. They remain highly innovative, but are so within the framework of the humanistic enterprise system, demonstrating the compatibility of entrepreneurship with the principles of human capitalism. (Honda is particularly noted for a corporate culture that encourages free and radical thinking among its workers.) These companies are not the exceptions. Toshiba, Fujitsu, NEC, Sanyo, Sharp, Hitachi, Toyota, Nissan, Mitsubishi, Kawasaki, New Japan Steel, YKK, and Kyocera are but some of the other highly innovative *and* humanistic major firms in Japan.

4

HOW HUMAN
CAPITALISM EVOLVED

❑

The Impact of the American Occupation

Japan before World War II was an approximation of the monopoly capitalism predicted by Karl Marx in the nineteenth century rather than of the classical capitalism envisioned by Adam Smith with great optimism in the eighteenth. The country was still a semideveloped industrial state under an authoritarian regime, burdened by overpopulation and heavy military expenditures. The distribution of income and wealth was considerably skewed, the upper class of the rich and powerful coexisting with the poor and undernourished masses.

Under the antiunion government labor activists, without the legal right of collective bargaining, not infrequently had to endure harsh crackdowns by the police. In most workplaces there were few signs of harmonious industrial relations. Management and labor represented two distinct groups, the haves and the have-nots. The former often dealt with labor disputes highhandedly. Throughout the land there were pervasive underemployment and an industrial reserve army of the unemployed. At the peak of the firms' pyramids presided *zaibatsu* families who, by means of holding companies, effectively controlled most of the major industries in the nation.

In the prewar period there were some early developments that faintly anticipated the kind of changes to occur after World War II. None of them, however, has really manifested conscious and deliberate movements toward building a humanistic enterprise system.

In the 1920s heavy industry began to experiment with a new

system of providing skilled workers, then highly scarce, with a long-term employment guarantee as a way of securing a steady and sufficient supply of their skills. This is said to have been the genesis of the lifetime-employment system, a main component of postwar Japanese-style management. Thanks to the country's late industrial development, which only began in the latter part of the nineteenth century, there were few established guilds, external to the firms, on which industry could depend in acquiring a supply of acutely needed skilled workers. To cope with the situation many firms were compelled to train workers in-house, with the expectation that they would stay with the same firm after their training. This practice foreshadows the institutionalization of the internal labor market under the postwar managerial system.

There were mild reforms within the *zaibatsu* structure before the war. Some old *zaibatsu* modified their exclusive reliance on holding companies and began to go public for equity financing because, given the rapid pace of capital formation, they were unable to raise enough capital through traditional means alone. The Mitsui holding company started to hire senior managers who were unrelated to the family, departing from the convention of filling executive positions only with family members. The monolithic standing of the old *zaibatsu* was challenged and weakened by the rise of new *zaibatsu* who freely sold their shares in the open stock market instead of holding them internally. The private monopoly power of *zaibatsu* was reduced during the late 1930s as their business was increasingly placed under state control and regulation as part of preparation for the war.

The wartime regime founded the Industrial Patriotic Society, charged with the task of organizing the enterprise-based unions throughout the country as a means of boosting the wartime morale and productivity of industrial workers. The society advocated hard work, cooperation, sacrifice, perseverance, community service, assistance to families of the drafted, and the like, all in the name of patriotism. At the end of the war the society was dissolved, but the administrative apparatus, experience, and know-how related to union activity at the firm level remained. Some observers have argued that the society unwittingly enhanced the prospect of popularizing the enterprise union as the representative form of organized labor after the war.

After the war, during the five-year period of American occupation in Japan, the country experienced radical changes in its legal, political, economic, and social systems. The occupation's central objective, after demilitarizing Imperial Japan, was to transform the country into a free, open, democratic society in America's image. A series of far-reaching reforms was introduced and executed. A parliamentary form of political democracy was instituted, replacing the old constitutional monarchy. Prolabor laws were passed, giving workers the right to organize and to bargain collectively with management. An antimonopoly law—the first of its kind in Japanese history and patterned after U.S. antitrust laws—was introduced to safeguard against the reemergence of monopoly capitalism. And, perhaps most significant from the standpoint of human capitalism, the *zaibatsu* system was dissolved. In the judgment of the U.S. policy planners the symbiotic coalition of the state and *zaibatsu* was the main cause of Japanese imperialism, and therefore a thorough destruction of the *zaibatsu* establishment was necessary.

The U.S. authorities began by making the holding companies illegal and ordering *zaibatsu* families to sell their stocks to the companies they had previously controlled, to employees of those companies, and to residents of localities where the companies were situated. Then they purged all the senior executives of the *zaibatsu* firms and prohibited them from assuming important positions during the occupation. With the advent of the Cold War there was some policy reversal; the *zaibatsu* dissolution, radical as it was, was not implemented as far as had originally been intended for fear that this might unduly weaken Japanese industry, making the country an unwanted burden to the United States at a time when Japan's industrial strength could be a useful asset in America's anticommunist strategy in the Far East. Nonetheless, the *zaibatsu* establishment as it had existed in prewar Japan vanished for good.

There are ironies in the story. The economic section of U.S. General Headquarters in Tokyo was filled with New Deal enthusiasts who found themselves in the position of being able to do practically anything they wanted in the occupied country, including radical economic reforms of a sort they might only have dreamed about back home. Yet, what they were trying to accomplish in Japan was to build a competitive, liberal capitalism mixed with strong American-style industrial unionism, not to lay the groundwork for "human capitalism" to rise and flourish later.

In fact, there were conservative members of Congress with a fundamental faith in the rights of capitalists who were disturbed by the extent of trust busting taking place in occupied Japan, and they wrote letters of protest to General Douglas MacArthur. Interestingly, MacArthur, a staunch conservative himself, resisted their protests.

Without the war and the American occupation, in all probability Japan would be a very different economic society today. It would probably be a nation under an authoritarian regime, heavily armed and dominated by monopoly capital, a society in which people would not fully enjoy basic human rights and freedoms and management and labor would maintain uneasy industrial relations filled with tension and suppressed hostility. Given the dominance of vested interests, attempted internal reforms would have been severely limited. In fact, human capitalism actually has American origins; the United States served as midwife at the birth.

Postwar Unionism

Enterprise unions became the popular form of organized labor in Japan after World War II and, as we have seen, an integral element of the humanistic enterprise system. Still, there is little to suggest that the spread of this particular kind of union in postwar Japan was inevitable. Article 28 of the new constitution guarantees "the right of workers to organize and to bargain and act collectively," but it does not stipulate what sort of union should be organized. The type of democratic labor organization foreseen and encouraged by the occupation authorities was the American-style industrial union. The main concern of Japanese labor activists, most of whom were leftist ideologues, was also to foster industrial unionism and to build a powerful national federation of labor organizations to confront management.

In the United States management-sponsored, paternalistic "company" unions were in vogue during the 1920s. The movement toward enterprise-level unionism in America, however, was disrupted by the Great Depression. From the base of company unions an industrial union was organized in the steel industry, and the trend began to spread to other industries. The prolabor Wagner Act of 1935 legitimatized collective bargaining and laid out the legal foundation on which the formidable industrial unionism was to grow in subsequent years.

The labor situation in prewar Japan was quite different. The state was generally antiunion, and its stance against leftist unions was intensified during the 1930s as the nation trod the road to fascism. Japanese labor had little time or opportunity to experience industrial unions. The war created a vacuum in the fragile and disconnected movement. Had there been much industrial unionism in prewar Japan, it is not improbable that after the war industrial unions with their adversarial stance against management would have become the mainstream of labor movements there.

In the years immediately following the war labor movements in Japan were in a state of utter chaos. The occupation authorities liberated the movements, but the labor activists were generally socialists or communists determined to destroy Japanese capitalism. Management was almost totally inexperienced when it came to confrontational collective bargaining. There was frequent discord between management and unions, as well as between unions operating within the same firm, and violence was not uncommon. (If the experiences of this period are any guide, incidentally, the idea that cooperativeness is inherent to Japanese social psychology is revealed to be total nonsense.)

For the majority of workers, however, the grave concern of the day was sheer survival. The entire nation had been thoroughly destroyed by the war. Food, housing, clothing, and everything else were in critically short supply. Workers were lucky just to find a job, any job. They knew that if they lost it, it would be nearly impossible to find another one elsewhere. They also understood that if their company failed, they and their families would starve. Realizing that survival was closely tied to the fate of the firm, they began to develop a sense of solidarity with their employer. For rank-and-file workers practically all management-labor problems were firm based or firm specific rather than industry oriented. Consequently, to them an enterprise union, not an industrial union, was the logical and sensible choice.

There is nothing inherently pacific or cooperative about an enterprise union. It can be as adversarial vis-à-vis management as an industrial union. In fact there were numerous instances of enterprise unions highly radicalized by leftist activists. What most likely happened is that the workers came to prefer the enterprise union for its rationality, and both management and labor gradually learned through trial and error to cooperate with each other for mutual survival (Table XIV in Appendix). As the humanistic enterprise system slowly evolved, the enterprise union was bound to become an inseparable component of that system.

The Managerial Revolution

It is a common lesson of business history that family-owned firms are fated to have relatively short longevity. Typically, an individual, driven by fervent entrepreneurship and an obsessive desire to build a personal fortune, starts, and succeeds in, a business venture. As the founder of the business reaches retirement age, some of his children, chosen for their apparent managerial acumen, take control of the family empire. But usually all that the second generation can accomplish is to hold on to the empire that was already built by the first generation. Members of the third generation, having grown in the comfort of personal opulence, are apt to lack sufficient drive or desire to continue the business, and thus begins the decline and fall of the family empire.

A family-owned enterprise, as it reaches its peak, faces a choice between preserving family control, with its risk of failure, and hiring competent professional managers from outside the family. Many families would naturally choose the latter. At the same time an increasing number of family owners, unable to finance further expansion of their businesses out of family funds alone, begin to issue and sell new shares of their stock in the open market, laying the groundwork for the coming of modern, large, publicly held corporations run by a new class of professional managers.

In America the managerial revolution—the separation of control from ownership of the firm—is said to have occurred around the turn of the century, after many decades of gradual change in the structure of corporate ownership. In sharp contrast the managerial revolution in Japan occurred suddenly, as part of the radical transformation of the country under the occupation. As the executives of the *zaibatsu* firms were purged by the American authorities and disappeared from the scene, the young executives replacing them found themselves almost completely free of outside capitalists' control. But while enjoying this freedom, the new managers had to face the unfamiliar problem of collectively bargaining with a union that had often been radicalized and confrontational during the early postwar years. The building of harmonious industrial relations was a joint learning experience, no doubt eased by the fact that the new managers, themselves former employees, had risen from the ranks (unlike the *zaibatsu* executives).

If the cooperative management-labor relationship was a product of conscious learning efforts by the parties concerned, the same is true for the institutionalization of lifetime employment. In the 1950s and even during the early 1960s, most firms did not yet thoroughly practice the Japanese-style management system, and layoffs were not uncommon. Through hard and bitter experiences, however, management learned that a quick layoff may be a rational act to enhance short-run efficiency of the firm but can have a devastatingly adverse effect on the firm in the long run. Most of the major, long-lasting, and extremely costly strikes in the 1950s and 1960s were caused by mass layoffs at depressed firms in coal, steel, and other industries. Management learned the hard way the virtue of a no-layoff policy, as it boosted workers' morale and productivity. Slowly, the firms began to adopt the lifetime-employment system as an implicit element of the employment contract. Expansion of a highly motivated and integrated work force in the leading sectors of the economy, thanks to this system, significantly contributed to Japan's accelerated growth, which in turn led to wider adoption of the system.

A late starter in economic development is said to have an advantage over an early starter because the former can quickly borrow advanced technology from the latter instead of developing it internally from scratch. Japanese firms have been noted for their "improvement" engineering, i.e., improving technology borrowed from the West before applying it to product development. What is true for engineering technology should also be true for management sciences.

In the 1950s American industry enjoyed a position of supremacy. In the rest of the world there was wide speculation that there must necessarily be a causal connection between industrial supremacy and the management system in America. What many Japanese firms were interested in at the time was not the abstract design of the humanistic enterprise system as such but emulation of the American-style management system. In the early 1960s there was a great "American management boom" in Japan, featuring numerous publications on the subject translated from English and religiously studied by the Japanese. Many firms did try to directly adopt American-style scientific management techniques, with emphasis on functionalism and job specialization. Through trial and error they accepted some aspects of the American system and rejected or modified others to suit their purpose.

The steel industry, for example, once actively applied job-specialization principles to its operations. Amid its rapid expansion, however, the industry was unable to build a corps of trained specialists quickly enough. So it began to delegate supervisory and inspection responsibilities to production workers, including job rotation and localized decision-making systems.

/ Evolution of the new management system in postwar Japan thus began with the introduction and emulation of the American-style management system. Innovative managerial experiments continued throughout the 1960s. It was only in the 1970s that Honda, Sony, Matsushita, YKK, Kyocera, and other leading firms started to develop their own, solidly people-oriented management philosophy, principles, techniques, and conventions, and it was this development that simultaneously led to the evolution and spread of human capitalism — just as the management system that became popular in eighteenth century England eventually induced the evolution of classical capitalism./

The Organized Capital Market

For most ordinary Japanese the stock market has not been an easily approachable place. They have kept their money in bank deposits and postal savings for convenience and safety. Especially during the early postwar years people were too poor to indulge themselves in a highly speculative form of investment. In fact, the stock market has been rather hostile to ordinary people. In the 1950s the investment trust (corresponding to mutual funds in America) became popular. During the stock-market crashes of 1961 and 1964–65, however, many individuals who had invested in the trusts suffered large capital losses. The market-stabilization measures undertaken by the monetary authorities required the trusts' portfolio to include stipulated amounts of national bonds and public-utilities shares, making investment trusts less attractive for most individual investors. While capital gains are tax exempt, dividends are taxable and have tended to be small, not reflecting profits of the firms. The regulated broker's fees have been high and regressive, to the disadvantage of small investors. Japanese households have historically held more fixed assets (house, land, etc.) than financial assets, one reason being that the large severance pay is illiquid and nontransferable until one reaches retirement age.

Given the underdevelopment of the stock market, debt financing became the primary means of raising funds for large corporations to execute their ever-increasing plant and equipment investments as the nation's economy completed its postwar recovery and began a new course of rapid growth. Banks provided voluminous credit to the firms and at the same time invested in the firms' equity for coprosperity and mutual supervision, thus initiating a pattern of enterprise grouping, with a main bank symbiotically affiliated with a set of major manufacturing concerns.

In 1960 the gradual, measured liberalization of trade started. The government's pronouncement of capital liberalization, scheduled to begin in 1967, spread fear in business circles that many Japanese firms would be taken over by powerful Western firms equipped with abundant capital and superior technology. Such fear may or may not have been justified; nevertheless, the major firms in each enterprise group began to practice mutual stockholding as a way of blocking off hostile mergers by foreign firms, adding to the growing trend of institutional investment. During the 1970s, in order to avoid diseconomies of scale and to effectively adjust to the rapid structural changes in industry, leading firms frequently spun off small firms as equity-sharing subsidiaries, which further added to the weight of institutional (as opposed to individual) investment in the country.

A key element of the humanistic enterprise system is that management of the humanistic firm is free of outside capitalists' unwanted influence and is capable of making autonomous decisions. This condition has been met in the context of enterprise grouping, whereby the firm heavily borrows from its main affiliated bank, which, given its own stake in the borrowing firm, is duty bound to support and conform to the long-term growth orientation of the firm. In the past decade, the firm-bank relationship has been visibly changing. After years of extraordinary performance and expansion many leading firms have accumulated enormous amounts of internal savings, so that they are far less dependent on banks for investment funds. While banks have been compelled to diversify their financial services into consumer credit, real estate, securities, overseas business, and other nontraditional areas, firms have increasingly been financing their new investments with their own internal funds. Having graduated from the earlier phase of debt financing, the humanistic firms now sustain their freedom and autonomy of decision making on the basis of their newly gained self-financing capacity.

The Nonideological Society

In the abstract most of us would agree that the basic values and attributes of the humanistic enterprise system—sharing, participation, cooperation, the recognition of humans as intellectual and psychological beings, and the view of the firm as an economic as well as social organization—transcend a specific society or historical period. The question then arises: Why hasn't such a system evolved in other parts of the world to the degree that it has in postwar Japan?

One obvious answer is that the vested interests, institutional rigidities, and inertia of old traditions form a hard wall of resistance to any radical change that would threaten the status quo. It took Japan a total defeat in the war and major surgery performed by the occupation authorities to become fertile ground for the seeds of human capitalism. But this does not explain the case of Germany, which also lost the war, suffered thorough destruction, and was occupied by foreign powers with similar objectives. Nor does it explain Italy and Great Britain, two countries that experienced extensive war destruction and had a good opportunity to introduce major economic reforms after the war, nor even the United States, which was badly shaken by the Great Depression.

Japan is said to be a nonideological society, and this may have much to do with the birth of human capitalism there. A persistent theme in Japanese traditional thought is that all things human, including beliefs, are ephemeral and subject to changes along with the tides of history. Of course, to say that nothing in life lasts forever is a platitude. The point is that their traditional belief is one of no belief; Japanese by and large feel uncomfortable with the issue of "ideology."

Ideology, or its absence, is a double-edged sword. A strong belief can move a mountain, stir human emotions, and mobilize millions toward a common cause. It may become the solid foundation of a great civilization and accomplish many worthy goals. The danger of ideology is that it may degenerate into a dogma that induces tunnel vision, a biased view instead of an enlightened grasp of the whole truth. A belief strongly held implies that all others who do not share the same belief are necessarily wrong. Hence, ideology encourages a confrontational stance in dealing with life's problems.

Nonideology, in essence, means healthy skepticism, open-mindedness, a belief in nonbelief, a conscious nonacceptance of absolute belief of any sort with awareness that any belief may lose its relevance contextually or historically. In short, it is a form of pragmatism, which leans toward whatever works and makes sense in reality, instead of what is correct in terms of some abstract, presupposed principles. On the other hand, nonideology may become a source of indecision, ambiguity, arbitrariness, amorality, and inability to make crucial but controversial decisions.

From the Japanese perspective Western civilization appears highly ideological. It produced both capitalism and socialism, which each developed its own strong ideology. In the twentieth century the conflict between the two ideologies culminated in the Cold War between the United States and the Soviet Union, with each side seemingly willing to risk annihilating the entire human race in defense of its truth.

For better or for worse neither Adam Smith nor Karl Marx was a Japanese. Capitalism, transplanted to Japan from the West in the nineteenth century, did not become a deep-rooted ideology. Had it done so, the economic system that emerged in postoccupation Japan would probably have been a new capitalism, reformed for greater freedom and competitiveness, but nevertheless the same capitalism as before the war in terms of its fundamental orientation. In the absence of ideological pull something unanticipated by the U.S. occupation authorities or anyone else started to happen. Through trial and error the firms gradually constructed a new people-oriented enterprise system. The capitalistic style of management-labor relations was dropped upon discovery that it was counterproductive to both parties. Radical unionism became unpopular because unions learned that though it was correct in terms of leftist ideology, it would not provide a practical solution to the problems they had to deal with. At the same time the firms did not possess a bible of human capitalism to follow, since no one had written such a convenient handbook. Rather, the humanistic enterprise system slowly evolved and assumed its shape out of the pragmatism of both management and workers.

The Future of Human Capitalism

Over a century ago Karl Marx predicted that capitalism would soon collapse under its own weight of inner contradictions, and would be replaced by socialism, an interim system that would usher in the era of communism, the final stage of historic human progress where the class struggle withers away and people live in peace and harmony. He took pains to insist that his was the theory of scientific socialism, not to be confused with utopian socialism, varieties of which abounded in his time.

In retrospect it seems clear that, contrary to his claim, he was very much a part of the nineteenth-century tradition of utopianism. His account of a communist society remained vague and impressionistic, and did not provide any specific formula for the legal, political, economic, and social institutions that would assure the emergence and preservation of a communal world totally free of human conflicts and exploitation. With all due respect to his intellectual genius, it is by now a fair verdict to declare, especially after the electrifying events of 1989 in Eastern Europe, that he was largely wrong about his predictions regarding the fall of capitalism and what was to happen thereafter.

Capitalism is a dynamic and efficient system insofar as production of goods and services goes, but it has not been able to dissolve the issues of alienation of industrial workers and of inequities in the distribution of income and wealth. Thus we face a dilemma, in that neither socialism nor capitalism appears to be an adequate solution for the contemporary world. Textbooks on the subject are of little help, as they continue to hold that these two systems are the only alternatives available.

We believe, however, that human capitalism offers a viable third way. It is not an abstract theory, but a system that has already been tested in a major economy in the world and has demonstrated its capacity to generate industrial productivity. It is based on sensible values and rational principles, and encourages the making of a competitive yet egalitarian society.

Human capitalism is no more a "Japan" phenomenon than capitalism, born in eighteenth-century England, is an "English" phenomenon. It happened to evolve in postwar Japan because of the presence of a right set of circumstances at that particular time and place. Given favorable conditions the same or a similar economic system would have emerged elsewhere at a different time (and, as we have seen, the United States played a crucial role in its birth). The system embraces the principles of freedom, equality, and industrial democracy that are essentially Western, rather than traditionally Japanese, values.

The logic of the birth of a system is not identical to the logic of its growth. If the system born (whether political, economic, or religious) is irrational and culture bound, it is destined to be a local phenomenon. If it is rational or has universal appeal, it will grow and spread beyond the particular place and time of its birth. Capitalism happened to emerge in eighteenth-century England, but it did not remain an exotic system practiced only in the British isles. On the contrary, it soon began to reach many corners of the globe, because, compared with the available alternatives, it was a rational, workable, and appealing system.

When we glance at the long sweep of history, we observe that past economic systems by and large were built on logic, as if people did not matter. In the premodern era a handful of individuals belonging to the privileged landowner class could influence the lives of millions of serfs and ordinary people. With the Industrial Revolution came capitalism, a system that gives owners of the firm inordinate power to subjugate the working class to machines and capital. In this century socialism, a system intended to solve the inherent problems of capitalism, arose and spread to many areas of the world. But socialism, it turned out, merely transfers monopoly power from capitalists to the state, and the state becomes the new oppressor of the masses.

As we move to the close of this century, there are clear signs, both in the East and the West, of yearning for an economic system under which people matter and can exercise their rights to determine their own destiny. In the twenty-first century we shall most probably witness the worldwide spread of new economic systems that are neither capitalistic nor socialistic but have the common central characteristic of people orientation. If this assessment of the global trend is correct, we then realize that the importance of human capitalism lies in its being the forerunner of what is likely to come in the next century.

No social institutions last forever. A system may begin rationally in the context of its time and place. Over time it will develop inner contradictions, or, as circumstances change, what used to be rational principles will become obsolete and irrational, setting the stage for its eventual decline. At present human capitalism looks to be the rational solution to the common problems of contemporary industrial society. But it is no exception to the law of impermanence. In the future it is bound to develop its own problems. For example, organized market competition alone may not provide sufficient discipline to prevent the management-worker coalition from fostering certain detrimental modes of behavior. Or a group of humanistic firms may conspire to form an implicit quasi-monopoly powerful enough to circumvent the antimonopoly law. It is too early to speculate, however, if or when these and other problems of human capitalism will arise.

5

THE QUESTION
OF CULTURE

❑

Trouble with the Culture Model

It has been fashionable for Western observers of the Japanese economy to approach the subject from what might be called the "culture model." The common theme of the model is that Japan's economic performance is to a large extent a product of Japanese culture, which is believed to be very different from Western culture; therefore, Japan cannot easily be emulated by the West.

What do we mean by culture? The dictionary usually defines it as "the sum total of ways of living built up by a group of human beings, which is transmitted from one generation to another." But, following this definition, culture covers practically everything that touches human existence—clothing, shelter, child rearing, schooling, religion, manners, mores, conventions, love, marriage, death, family, kinship, rituals, and so on. Indeed, one inherent problem with the culture model is that it tends to degenerate into tautology, explaining everything and nothing. If you argue that the major attributes of Japanese culture are the right stuff for accelerated economic growth, and take this as the main source of Japan's economic success, in effect you are saying that the Japanese economy has grown thanks to the way the Japanese behave, which is determined by their culture. In other words, they behave like Japanese because they are Japanese—not a particularly revealing proposition.

The conventional definition of culture gives the impression that each culture is constant and timelessly transmitted from one generation to another. This impression is misleading and often false. The culture of a group of people, a country, or a region does change over time, sometimes surprisingly fast in the contemporary world. In America, for example, the sexual mores and perception of women's role in society have changed considerably since the 1950s.

Another misleading impression provided by the common definition of culture is that it is prone to be particular and irrational, and hence the attributes of one culture cannot easily be transmitted to another. But certain aspects of culture *do* travel across time and space. Each culture is unique in some respects, and a synthesis of other cultures in other respects. Twenty years ago eating raw fish was considered a daring, if not barbaric, act in America; today sushi is enjoyed by thousands of Americans. In the realm of human customs what is irrational is often merely a matter of being unaccustomed. On the whole, Americans seem to be deeply concerned with housekeeping, as witnessed by the proliferation of commercials on floor wax, detergent, and other house-cleaning materials; if so, it strikes the Japanese as irrational that Americans, unlike Japanese, do not remove their shoes as they enter their houses. The culture model has a tendency to emphasize the particularity of a culture under observation and to deemphasize, if not ignore, cross-cultural similarities that may in fact exist.

Another pitfall of the culture model is that it unwittingly encourages the view that people in each country are culturally homogeneous, i.e., a common set of cultural attributes is presumed applicable to most, if not all, people in question. The result is a "national character" argument, which says in effect that when you have seen one Japanese (or American), you have seen them all. Needless to say, such an argument will distort, rather than clarify, the truth, as it conveniently disregards the enormous diversities that may be found among members of society.

According to the culture model Japanese workers are loyal

to their employers in the manner samurai were loyal to their masters, and peasants to the local lords, in the feudal era that lasted through the latter part of the nineteenth century. Presumably Japanese feudalism was so intense and long lasting that loyalty became a mental reflex that has survived decades of modernization and even persists today. The workers develop a deep sense of belonging to their firm, and out of a feeling of duty and obligation they do not readily quit in search of a few more bucks at another firm. This obviously helped the firms and hence the economy—so goes the argument—toward rapid industrial growth of the nation.

Such an argument is a caricature at best, is inconsistent with Western economic theory, and is contradicted by historical facts. If workers stay on with the same firm to fulfill their sense of loyalty, and management reciprocates with its paternalistic guarantee of lifetime employment security regardless of workers' aptitude and performance records, the result predicted by Western economic theory will be a reduction in interfirm mobility of labor, a misallocation of resources, and efficiency loss for the economy, retarding the process of industrialization. In the late nineteenth century and around the turn of the twentieth, the Japanese labor market resembled the contemporary American counterpart. Job hopping was common, and absenteeism rampant. Many firms adopted the system of paying wages on different days to different workers because if all wages were paid on the same day so many workers would not report to work the next day. Following the culture model's reasoning, workers at that time, which was shortly after the end of the feudal period, should have been far more loyal to their employers than today.

The same model should logically argue that American workers frequently change jobs and experience little compunction about leaving present employers because their culture does not prize a sense of loyalty. A better explanation seems to be, however, that in the context of American capitalism workers perform certain specified jobs at the firm as a matter of contract; it is well understood between management and labor that workers do not belong to the firm and management may lay them off any day as deemed desirable by the firm. In such a context there is no more rationality in workers' feeling loyal to their employers than in citizens' remaining loyal to their country when the government announces that it may any time revoke their citizenship without due process of law.

People in most countries develop varying degrees of loyalty on account of the nation-state system under which they must exist. One's nationality defines one's legal rights and obligations, which in turn condition what we can or cannot do inside our homeland and abroad. Under the nation-state system the lot of a stateless person in most cases is much worse than that of a person with a nationality. But if nation-states were totally to disappear from the earth and we had full freedom to move around the world without facing any legal barriers, it is doubtful that many of us would retain a sense of national identity or of loyalty to a particular state.

The culture model often cites the work ethic as an attribute of Japanese culture that has favored the country's economic growth. Other things being equal, a stronger work ethic leads to greater output and higher quality of what is produced, and self-evidently contributes to the nation's economic expansion. This argument may explain those industries that have grown tremendously in postwar Japan, such as steel, shipbuilding, automobiles, home appliances, consumer electronics, and so on, but fails to account for the noted depression of other industries like petrochemicals and nonferrous metals (particularly aluminum). The model does not explain why Japanese workers in the automobile industry are endowed with a strong work ethic, yet the same Japanese apparently lose it once they step into the petrochemical industry. While Japan led the world in shipbuilding for many years, the industry has been depressed since the mid-1970s. The model does not offer a clear account of why the work ethic of the workers in the shipbuilding industry suddenly weakened around 1975.

Harmony is another popular theme of the culture model. The Japanese are supposed to be harmonious people, and consequently, the model holds, industrial relations in Japan tend to be peaceful and cooperative rather than disharmonious and confrontational. It is true that Japanese society emphasizes the importance of harmony. Public speeches on varied occasions often take harmony as a theme for discussion. The popularity of harmony in social rhetoric, however, hardly proves that the people are spontaneously harmony loving. On the contrary, it may imply the opposite; perhaps society stresses it because it is lacking in fact.

Every society has different faces, and, depending on which face one looks at, one is left with a different impression. It took years to build Narita International Airport, the main gate to Tokyo, because of radical and sustained opposition by leftist groups and local farmers. To this day Narita has only two runways, the government having been unable to construct the third one in the face of continuing opposition. Many foreigners, arriving at Narita for the first time, are shocked to see armed antiriot police guarding the gates to the airport; this does not quite match the conventional image of a harmonious Japan. Their preconceived image may be further shaken when they learn that strikes do occur in the country, and that during the early postwar years violent and prolonged strikes were not uncommon.

One commonly cited source of alleged Japanese harmony is rice farming, which requires close and frequent coordination and cooperation among villagers for seeding, planting, and harvesting. As they worked their paddies together, the culture model argues, they developed over the centuries a firm sense of harmony, which became a reflex of the Japanese mind. What the model does not mention is that Japanese agricultural history is filled with tales of bitter water disputes among rice farmers, who fought for access to the limited local supply of water.

The *kanban* system (alternatively called the "just-in-time" or "zero-inventory" system) has been identified as a remarkable aspect of the Japanese automobile industry. The system manages to reduce inventory to near zero through streamlined

and highly integrated networking of the automobile manufacturers and layers of parts suppliers. (The assembler of parts
orders them as needed, and the supplier delivers them just in
time.) It has been suggested that the system to a large extent
is a fruit of Japanese culture, since it requires a high spirit of
coordination and harmonious work habits among assemblers
and subcontractors. The fact of the matter is that the Toyota
engineers acquired the initial idea for the *kanban* system when
they were visiting supermarkets in America and examining
their inventory-control methods. The company's first attempt
to develop and introduce the system met with the union's bitter
opposition. It took Toyota Motor Corporation twenty years of
trial and error to perfect it.

The culture model has fondly described the Japanese as a
harmonious people, owing to their exceptional homogeneous-
ness in comparison with other societies in the world. They
think and act alike and can communicate with one another easily; and thus their homogeneity has contributed to the cultiva-
tion of diligence, loyalty, cooperativeness, and other favorable
factors in Japan's economic growth.

We shall leave aside the question whether homogeneity per
se is a positive or negative element in the nation's economic
dynamism. A group of people who think and act alike may
develop complacency, intellectual laxity, and a love of
conformity, while a heterogeneous society may encourage
innovation, inventiveness, creativity, competition, and
entrepreneurship.

A more serious problem is the ambiguity of the term
homogeneity. It usually refers to such criteria as language, ethnicity, religion, culture, history, and philosophy, but depending on which criteria are used or how much weight is given to
a particular criterion, the same country may be declared to be
more or less homogeneous than others. America is often cited
as an example par excellence of heterogeneous society on account of its ethnic diversity. Yet the country has one language
and a wide commonality of belief in political democracy and
the free enterprise system. Therefore, America may be de-

scribed as a highly unified, homogeneous society as far as language and political-economic thought are concerned. It certainly is more homogeneous than Yugoslavia, a nation noted for its linguistic, ethnic, and cultural diversity.

Japan is perceived as a homogeneous society on the basis of its common language, the absence of large ethnic minorities, and a common culture. By the same criteria we may judge Italy, Holland, Sweden, or Finland no less homogeneous than Japan. It is not difficult to assemble examples or counterexamples to prove or disprove the correlation, if not causation, between homogeneity and the economic success of a country (or a region). Switzerland enjoys the world's highest per capita income despite its linguistic diversity. The Hawaiian economy is well developed notwithstanding its accentuated ethnic diversity. The Argentinian economy has been faltering in spite of the commonality of its language and religion. The Polish economy has been stagnant, while the country is homogeneous in terms of language, religion, and ethnicity. And so on.

An interesting example is Korea, a nation that resembles Japan in many respects. It has one language, is ethnically homogeneous, has a long history as a centralized state, is endowed with a relatively small geographic space, has actually developed less local color than Japan, and was devastated by the Korean War. Despite these similarities, however, the humanistic enterprise system has not emerged in Korea. Instead, owner-capitalists and family-controlled businesses are common, interfirm mobility of labor is high, and the seniority-based wage system is unpopular. Koreans in general do not view the firm as a quasi-familial, communal organization. They prefer free movement, choice, and the establishment of business and personal connections with people who are not necessarily co-workers in the same company.

Culture and Economic Theory

Since, as we have seen, the sociological culture model only tends to confuse the issues, what happens when we apply economic theory? The mainstream economics taught in universities and colleges in the West has its origin in Adam Smith's *The Wealth of Nations* (published in 1776), the book that, according to many, first established economics as an objective social science, instead of the subjective intellectual discipline—a mixture of economics, ethics, and moral philosophy—that it had been in earlier times. Smith's thoughts gave rise, during the next century, to an elegant body of literature known as the "English classical school." Toward the close of the nineteenth century its tenets were merged with those of the so-called marginalist school, and the outcome of that merger was "neoclassical economics."

The neoclassical theory is mainly concerned with analysis of the free-enterprise economy. In essence it is a modeling of Western-style capitalistic firms. Each individual economic agent—a capitalist, manager, worker, or consumer—is assumed to be a *Homo economicus* in constant pursuit of self-interest. Oddly, the neoclassical theory of the firm dwells mostly on market structures—monopoly, duopoly, oligopoly, monopolistic competition, perfect competition, etc.—and how they affect the firm's profit-maximizing strategy, and says little about what really goes on inside the firm. The theory conveys the image of the firm as a mechanistic black box with two holes, one for inputs and another for outputs. Those inside are invisible, faceless beings performing specified functions. Workers come and go with no apparent emotions as management adjusts the optimum level of employment.

There is much confusion about the universality of neoclassical economics. Presumably the theory is a modeling of capitalism as it has evolved in the West, and therefore embraces, in one way or another, biases of Western culture. But the serious practitioners of the craft believe that it is free of cultural biases. They claim that culture is a datum to be taken as given, and the model can easily incorporate a different culture simply by changing its parameters accordingly. The less serious practitioners are not even sure, however, how closely the theory explains the actual behavior of the firms operating under Western-style capitalism.

When Western neoclassical economists look at the Japanese economy, they knowingly or unknowingly employ the neoclassical model as their frame of reference. To their mind, conditioned to assume the impersonality of the market and the mechanistic mode of production as the norm, the organized market and participatory management of the firm seem peculiar. Many of them, consequently, conclude that Japan is an anomaly, a capitalism with some particular twists of Japanese culture. But to call the second largest economy in the world an anomaly is a case of outmoded cultural imperialism.

For the past two hundred years major industrial growth has occurred within Western capitalistic countries. Hence the tendency to assume that Western culture is necessarily rational and consistent with the principles of industrialism, and culture of the non-Western world, where economic development has been retarded, must be inimical to modern industrialization. But one lesson of Japan's postwar economic performance is that Western culture, aside from what it really means, is a neither necessary nor sufficient condition for modern economic growth.

Individualism versus Groupism

The issue of individualism versus groupism is a topic that frequently appears in the discussion of things Japanese. It is said that Westerners are individualistic whereas Japanese are group oriented, and this alleged difference is promoted as a major source of the distinctions in patterns of economic and social development between the West and Japan. This theme has been repeated so often that it has become conventional wisdom for many observers of Japan, and has consequently gone unexamined.

Discussion of the issue often is filled with confusion and inconsistency. A popular opinion holds that the group orientation of the Japanese has contributed to the nation's economic growth, inasmuch as it encourages harmonious industrial relations and cooperative work efforts in the firms. According to this view, then, groupism is good and individualism bad for modern industrialism. Yet not long ago, before the rise of the Japanese technological superstate, individualism, which promotes creativity, innovation, and competitiveness, was identified as a positive factor in Western economic growth, implying that groupism is a negative factor. More recently, we hear that the excess of individualism is causing deterioration of the work ethic in America and hence the decline of American industry. All we learn from such reasoning is that individualism and/or groupism may be good and/or bad for the nation's economy depending on time and place—a comforting thought for those curious about the social psychology of economic growth.

One problem is that the terms are used loosely and arbitrarily. For instance, a common understanding of the term *individualism* is that each person makes his or her own decisions and takes responsibility for the consequences of those decisions rather than depending on others to cope with personal problems. There is, however, a good deal of disparity between theory and practice. To give a few examples: Many Americans who normally uphold the principle of individual sovereignty are quick to blame society or government once they face personal misfortunes such as unemployment, homelessness, or poverty. A significant percentage of Americans choose to be on welfare rather than to work, since, given the way the welfare system operates, being on welfare brings them more net disposable income than working; whereas if they were spontaneously and autonomously individualistic they would, as a matter of principle, work rather than depend on the state for their personal welfare. And how are we to describe supposedly individualistic Americans who, while in military service, readily cooperate with and conform to the military command?

In business the philosophy of individualism is closely interlinked with the ideology of laissez-faire. Many American businesspeople publicly state their belief that government should leave the private firms alone. They argue that the free-enterprise system, which rewards the efficient and punishes the inefficient, is what keeps the nation's economy strong and productive. In practice, however, their behavior is often at odds with their professed creed. While they wholeheartedly endorse the doctrine of laissez-faire, they will, without compunction, ask for government assistance once their own business gets into serious trouble, as did President Lee Iaccoca of Chrysler Corporation.

Similarly, there is much ambiguity about the term *groupism*. The often-heard statement "The Japanese are a group-oriented people" is usually made in a positive sense. But while it is true that the Japanese have a high propensity to form small private associations in organizing their lives, one outstanding characteristic of these groups is that members can be chillingly indifferent to those on the outside. It is not certain whether this sort of groupism, as it flourishes in the context of Japanese culture, can be identified as a positive source of industrial growth. Narrowly focused, it lacks a broad vision and elements of universality. It can hardly be viewed as a proper ideological foundation of a large industrial state, management of which requires wider, less personal, and less exclusionistic affiliations.

A popular image of the Japanese is that they possess a culturally conditioned reflex to put group interests before their personal interests. There is little convincing evidence to support such a notion, however. The Western media has fondly focused its attention on the scenes of Japanese factory workers singing their company anthem in unison before they start their day's work, presumably "evidence" of Japanese groupism. But the truth of the matter is that at the majority of Japanese firms workers do not sing their company song each morning. Indeed, Japanese visitors to the United States are impressed with the fact that there are so many occasions when Americans sing their national anthem—far more than in Japan. They may return home with the thought that Americans are more group oriented than Japanese, contrary to what they might have believed previously; or that Americans are group oriented toward their nation but not with respect to their employers.

The culture model would also argue that groupism is deeply rooted in Japanese history. It is hard to establish a strong connection, however, between the rise of the humanistic enterprise system in postwar Japan and the groupism that had presumably persisted over the past centuries. In the twelfth and thirteenth centuries it was fashionable for samurai to introduce themselves to the enemy before the start of a duel or to imprint their names on arrows in order to identify, after the battle, those responsible for the crucial killings. Such practices suggest that the warriors of medieval Japan were spirited individualists. Rice farming in traditional Japan is said to have nurtured the spirit of group enterprise; yet in Korea and Thailand, which also have a long history of rice farming, no similar enterprise systems have emerged.

Given its emphasis on absolute loyalty, austerity, sacrifice, devotion, duty, and uncompromising ethics, Bushido (the way of the samurai) has been cited as a probable origin of the cohesiveness of the Japanese work force. But in feudal Japan samurai accounted for five percent of the total population and were not permitted to engage in any form of commerce, a profession beneath their dignity. The business of a samurai was to swing swords, not cut deals. With the advent of modernization in the late nineteenth century, they lost their privileges, and many of them, out of necessity, became merchants, often failing miserably in a new, unfamiliar world. The Meiji Japanese expression *bushi no shoho*—samurai's way of commerce—connotes the lack of business acumen.

Even Confucianism has been mentioned as the source of Japanese firms' group dynamics. This is peculiar and farfetched reasoning: peculiar because the same Confucianism has been blamed for China's stagnation in the modern century; farfetched because Confucianism is a secular religion that originates in an ancient code of ethics written for a small elite of Chinese senior bureaucrats and state functionaries, and has little to do with entrepreneurship or the art of pecuniary ventures.

The moral of all this seems to be that the reasoning based on the individualism-versus-groupism dichotomy is not particularly useful in understanding enterprise dynamics. The two are not mutually exclusive, and the same people may be both individualistic and group oriented. Americans are perfectly capable of cooperating with others under many circumstances. They cooperate with other soldiers in war, with members of their families, with their neighbors, with affiliates of church or civic organizations, with their teammates in group sports. As they do so, they do not feel that they are violating the rule of individualism.

It was the West that invented the concept of nationalism. A majority of allegedly individualistic Westerners are loyal to their nation without feeling an excruciating contradiction as they lead an individually oriented life in other spheres of their existence. They have shown that they are capable of being group oriented with respect to their state while remaining individualistic in their workplace. That being so, they surely can perceive the possibility of a group-oriented enterprise system, even if they do not currently practice it.

Similarly, the notion that Japanese are groupistic is distorting and only half true. Many popular sports in contemporary Japan such as baseball, basketball, and soccer were invented in, and imported from, the West. Popular traditional sports and pastimes in Japan like sumo, judo, kendo, flower arrangement, and calligraphy are essentially individual activities. The Japanese, like any other people, behave individualistically or in groups depending on circumstances.

Self-Interest and Rational Behavior

As Adam Smith pointed out, self-interest is a constant in human nature that cuts across time and geographic space. Another such constant is that people everywhere act rationally toward enhancing their self-interest. Their specific acts, however, depend on particular circumstances. Rational behavior in one situation may be irrational in another. Independent professionals in contemporary America, where the work ethic is reportedly declining, work hard in pursuit of personal fortunes. It is not necessary to tell them to work hard or to threaten to punish their contrary behavior.

A third constant in human nature is that people everywhere need to compete as well as cooperate with others, in their own self-interest. As long as we live in society, we are destined to do so. There are many things that one person alone cannot accomplish at all, or cannot accomplish as well as when acting with others as a group. Spontaneously and willingly, people join a group and cooperate with other members of the group as long as it enhances their self-interest.

Workers in humanistic Japanese firms appear to have a strong sense of work ethic, teamwork, and loyalty to the company. Their attitude, however, has fundamentally little to do with their "culture": remember that their behavior was not so admirable during the early postwar years, to say nothing of the ubiquity of job-hopping in Meiji Japan. Rather, the behavior of workers at the humanistic firm is simply a rational response to the particular circumstance under which they work. There is a close link between their personal interest and that of the firm, and they must bear substantial costs if their firm fails. Consequently, it is only rational for them to work hard and cooperate with others toward enhancement of the firm's collective productivity. Their motives are no different from those of members of a small business partnership in contemporary America, who closely cooperate with each other because they share both the benefits and costs of their joint business.

At the same time management "needs" a strong work ethic among workers for the firm's survival, since the work force is internalized and management cannot readily lay off its members. Needless to say, management cannot impose the work ethic on workers through moral indoctrination. The only option available to it is to institutionalize the sharing of benefits and costs so that the workers themselves will spontaneously develop a strong work ethic in their own interest.

In the American firm the work ethic is more problematic. Employees do not belong to the firm, and there is neither participatory management nor significant sharing of benefits, so there is no rational reason for them to improve their work efforts. Most probably, they will take with them in leaving the firm the same attitude toward work that they had when entering it.

In an underdeveloped economy where labor is abundant and jobs are scarce, workers cultivate, on their own, a strong work ethic as a rational choice. If they do not work hard, they will be fired, and they and their families will pay a heavy price in deepening poverty. In contrast, modern, affluent society has a tendency to weaken the work ethic. High income, sufficient saving, social security, unemployment benefits, and the relative ease of finding another job with comparable pay considerably reduce the cost of losing a job. The lower cost of unemployment decreases the benefit of holding a strong work ethic. One may find genuine satisfaction in diligence for personal reasons, but that is an exception. Most workers lose economic incentive for sustaining a strong work ethic. In this sense the firms in an advanced society are thankless victims of the affluence of the society in which they operate. In the case of American firms, however, they partly have themselves to blame for the problem, because institutionally they have not equipped themselves to foster a spontaneous, self-generating work ethic among their workers.

The integrated internal labor market and the sharing of costs and benefits at the humanistic enterprise are institutional innovations that may reverse the trend of a declining work ethic in modern society. The humanistic firm is not content simply to go along with whatever personal work ethic new recruits may bring to the firm. Instead it makes deliberate efforts to assure that diligence becomes a rational behavioral trait on the part of its workers. The viability of the humanistic enterprise system rests on the simple proposition that people behave rationally in pursuit of their self-interest. Groupism as such is neither necessary nor sufficient for the working of the system.

6

RELATIONSHIP TO THE JAPANESE-STYLE MANAGEMENT SYSTEM

❑

The Management System

Any economic system may be defined in terms of its general principles, which are expressible in abstract language without reference to a particular culture, tradition, or history. In every economic system an enterprise system emerges whose working principles are consistent with the general characteristic of the economic system. When we look inside the firms operating under a given enterprise system, we witness the management system in action, a set of explicit or implicit rules conditioning and characterizing the manner in which the representative firm is actually managed on a day-to-day basis. Since the firm does not operate in a sociological vacuum, the management system tends, in one way or another, to embody specific cultural elements. While the United States, Great Britain, West Germany, and Italy are basically capitalistic economies, how each country's firms are managed reflects different traditions and historical backgrounds.

Inside the representative humanistic firm in Japan the so-called Japanese-style management system (JSMS) prevails. We might consider JSMS an adaptation of the abstract principles of human capitalism to the particular context of Japanese culture. If and when human capitalism is transplanted to other soils, it will predictably undergo modifications of itself to suit the specific constraints and requirements of different cultures, as has happened to capitalism in the course of its global spread following its birth in eighteenth-century England. Anything culture bound tends to be particular rather than universal, and therefore many aspects of the management system found in a country are not easily transferable to another culture. But this should not be confused with exportability of the principles of an economic system that are universal and rational.

What has commonly been understood as JSMS is the type of management system practiced by the large firms in the advanced sectors of the Japanese economy. The core elements of JSMS are: the lifetime-employment system *(shushin koyo seido),* seniority-based wages *(nenko joretsu),* and the enterprise union *(kigyobetsu kumiai).* Consensual decision-making, sharing, and enterprise welfare are also understood to be standard elements. The system emerged and became a well-developed, clearly identifiable institution after World War II; JSMS as such did not exist in prewar Japan. As we move from large to medium-sized and small firms, the system progressively loses its cohesion and is practiced less frequently. However, the main reason why smaller firms do not practice JSMS as commonly as larger ones is that they do not have sufficient resources to maintain it. Very often, when a small firm grows in size it tends to adopt the principles of JSMS. In Japanese society there is a widespread notion that JSMS represents a "natural" mode of managing the business firm. About twenty-five to thirty percent of the nation's total labor force works under well-developed JSMS. It should be noted, however, that those employed under JSMS are the best-trained and the most productive workers in the large, most technologically advanced firms operating in the strategically important sectors of the Japanese economy.

JSMS has been subject to different interpretations, depending on observers' perspectives. According to one school of thought JSMS is essentially a product of Japanese culture, and therefore is not readily transferable to other countries with different cultural backgrounds. A strong sense of loyalty to the firm, the propensity to view the firm as a quasi-familial organization, the ability and willingness to cooperate with other members of the group, are alleged to be attributes of Japanese culture; without them it is considered infeasible to sustain the viability of JSMS.

In the early postwar years the critics would often emphasize what was wrong with JSMS, from both neoclassical and Marxian perspectives. From the neoclassical viewpoint JSMS was an irrational system that violated the principles of a free and open market. The lifetime-employment system severely curtailed interfirm mobility of labor, resulting in suboptimal allocation of human resources. Similarly, seniority-based wages distorted the real costs of human inputs, and hence hindered the firm's internal efficiency. At the same time leftist observers attacked JSMS as an embodiment of the feudalistic ethos and capital's new subtle way of exploiting labor. The lifetime employment and seniority-based wages had succeeded in encamping labor within the firm and in weakening workers' sense of the class struggle under the illusion that they were members of one happy corporate family. According to the leftist view consensual and participatory management was in truth management by stress.

As Japan's economic growth continued in the 1960s, a new interpretation appeared, shifting its focus to what was right with JSMS. The new model argued that the neoclassical critique was at odds with facts; it was hard to believe that there was no connection between JSMS and Japan's economic success. It held that the Western capitalistic way was not the exclusive approach to economic development and growth, and that JSMS demonstrated that cultural variations were possible on the theme of industrial expansion. The firms under JSMS functioned well and efficiently because they organized their internal resources following rules that were consistent and compatible with the dictates and constraints of Japanese culture.

JSMS stayed intact during the course of accelerated economic growth, instead of disintegrating and absorbing Western-style free-market principles. On the other hand, in the West there has been a clear trend toward greater concern with employment security and cooperative management-labor relations. On the basis of these developments some observers maintain that JSMS, its cultural origins aside, actually is a forerunner of the forthcoming global trend toward which the Western-style management systems are slowly converging. ⏌

The Lifetime-Employment System

The expression "lifetime-employment system," which is closely associated with JSMS, is misleading in several ways. Contrary to what the term suggests, it is not an explicit employment contract unconditionally guaranteeing job security from the moment the employee joins the firm onward. Rather, it is an implicit agreement between the firm and its workers that management will pursue a minimum-layoff policy during hard times; in turn workers are expected to stay with the company over the long term. It also does not mean that workers remain employed until an advanced age. Under the system retirement comes early. Except for those on the executive track the mandatory retirement age, until recently, was fifty-five; it is now being shifted up to sixty. (Cynics have preferred to call it the "early-retirement system.") Further, some workers do quit, especially in the early years of employment, or are dismissed for their incompetence or misconduct.

At one level of perception the lifetime-employment system appears to be the embodiment of a culture that approaches the firm as a quasi-family. Management, out of its paternalistic concern for them, will not easily lay off workers, just as a father, even though hard pressed, would not think of abandoning members of his family. According to this perception the system is an attitude that can only be understood in the context of the underlying culture.

Paternalism might have facilitated formation of the lifetime-employment system in postwar Japan, but it is not the major factor in initiating and sustaining it—after all, the system as such was absent from prewar Japan. An early sign of it emerged in the beginning part of this century, in heavy industries that were still in an embryonic stage of development. Its intent, however, was to retain skilled workers who were then in critically scarce supply. By contrast, in America, generally perceived as a nonpaternalistic culture, career bureaucrats in government and tenured faculty in academia essentially live under a "lifetime-employment system."

The cultural interpretation notwithstanding, in several respects the lifetime-employment system is not paternalistic at all. Like the capitalistic firm the humanistic firm is there to make profits. It screens job applicants with utmost care in terms of schooling, personal traits, and aptitudes in order to pick the best, brightest, and most promising. Errors in judgment do occur, and the firm deals with unsatisfactory workers by not promoting them or giving them important assignments. Some quit voluntarily shortly after joining the firm; others leave later, having learned that they are unwanted by management. Occasionally the firm fires outright those who have critically misbehaved or committed criminal acts.

Lifetime employment does not mean that there is no competition inside the firm. On the contrary, under the system of slow promotion workers fight a long, hard battle against one another for higher positions. The system of slow promotion provides late bloomers with second and third chances, which only intensifies and prolongs intrafirm competition.

Under the lifetime-employment system workers retire at a relatively early age so that the work force as a whole will stay young, productive, and flexible. Given the seniority-based wage system, older workers, relative to their productivity, are overcompensated. From the firm's perspective, therefore, a relatively early retirement is economically rational, if not paternalistically correct. For the same reason, in a severe depression the firm may start to dismiss the oldest workers first, rather than the youngest ones. Under JSMS seniority is a determinant of compensation, but not of employment security, for the older members of the work force. The firm, however, commonly arranges matters so that many of its retirees will assume second-career opportunities in smaller, affiliated firms.

One factor peculiar to Japanese society tends to reinforce the working of the lifetime-employment system. Among the firms there is a tacit agreement not to hire workers from other firms, since those who quit on their own or are dismissed are deemed probably unstable, unreliable, and incapable. This may or may not be a reasonable assumption to make, but the agreement creates a powerful reputation effect that dissuades workers from shirking, as they are reminded of the high cost of departing from the present firm. The same agreement definitely discourages midcareer transfers to other firms. Those who wish to quit in the middle of their careers risk the costs of not being able to locate comparable or better jobs elsewhere.

There is a school of thought that the so-called lifetime-employment system is a mirage, a perception of reality rather than reality itself. In Japan, as in America, there is a lot of labor mobility among small and medium-size firms. Even among the large firms practicing JSMS a fair number of workers, especially young ones in the early phase of their careers, quit and move to other firms; the older workers are less prone to interfirm mobility. But essentially the same pattern prevails in America. It is a common phenomenon in America that, while young, workers frequently change jobs in search of the best available, locate the one to their liking, then stay with the same firm over a long period of time. According to this school of thought, depending on how one takes and compares statistics, many large, well-established firms in America practice a de facto lifetime-employment system in that, while there is no agreement as such on job security, the average American white-collar workers stay with the same firms about as long as Japanese white-collar workers. What is notable about the Japanese system, allegedly, is not so much the conspicuously long stay of the average worker with the same firm as the fact that the system has homogenized white- and blue-collar workers, with the latter becoming indistinguishable from the former in terms of their career pattern, long-term affiliation with the same firm, and development and accumulation of firm-specific skills.

Under the lifetime-employment system the personnel department plays an extremely important role in carefully and deliberately developing intrafirm human resources from a long-term perspective. The department is highly centralized in order to effectively execute its task of nurturing a well-integrated cooperative work force, in contrast to the substantially decentralized information and decision-making system within the same firm. Personnel assignments at all levels are made with thought given to their overall and long-term implications for the firm. The combination of a centralized personnel system with a decentralized information system under JSMS is the reverse of what is commonly observed in American firms. American-style management typically employs a vertical command system under which the information network is centralized, whereas the personnel department, given the firm's heavy reliance on the external labor market in recruiting new workers at all levels, tends to be decentralized, with hiring and firing decisions made locally by appropriate personnel managers.

Seniority-Based Wages

The compensation system under JSMS is commonly known as the "seniority-based wage system." As with lifetime employment, this expression is somewhat misleading. It does not mean that wages are determined solely or predominantly on the basis of seniority, but rather that seniority is a significant factor in calculating compensation.

Total compensation under JSMS equals the sum of contractual pay, various allowances, and semiannual bonuses. Contractual pay consists of basic pay, merit pay, and job-related pay. Of these basic pay, the largest of the three, refers to seniority-based wages, as its amount increases in proportion to the number of years worked at the firm. Merit pay is a variable compensation for a worker's meritorious performance. Job-related pay was introduced in the 1950s as an explicit element of the wage system, and was then hailed as a sign of the modernization of Japanese management methods. As the humanistic enterprise system grew and spread subsequently, however, job-related compensation became an increasingly awkward matter, since workers at the humanistic firms are generalists rather than specialists, and therefore it is nearly impossible to determine each worker's "job-related" pay.

Workers receive allowances for spouses, dependents, housing, and even commuting. These allowances originated in the early postwar period, when the nation was suffering from the scars of war and the average worker struggled for sheer survival. Housing, for example, was so scarce then that where to locate a residence was not a matter of choice. If a worker had to spend three hours commuting one way, it was because the distant house was the only one available. The firms were compelled to provide the allowances in order to sustain the minimum level of economic welfare of their employees. Times have changed, but the system of allowances has been preserved, an integral part of JSMS, though mainly as a symbolic gesture of egalitarianism. Besides these welfare-oriented allowances there is a regular allowance for overtime.

Bonuses are adjusted for individual merit and according to the financial condition of the firm. As noted earlier, in a good year they may be as large as four or five months' worth of regular wages. Semiannual adjustment of bonuses enables JSMS to operate under a flexible-wage system instead of the more constricting fixed-wage associated with American management.

The seniority-based wage system is, in a way, economically rational in the context of the internalized labor market. Workers stay with the same firm over a long period of time, learning and accumulating firm-specific skills. Consequently, the average worker's worth to the firm keeps increasing with time, and seniority-based wages may be interpreted as temporal allowances for the workers' steadily rising productivity. What may be true for the average worker, however, is certainly not true for all workers. It is also doubtful that a worker's overall productivity continues to increase in linear fashion until the very moment of retirement.

The system does serve as an effective incentive scheme to internalize human resources. It is one thing that JSMS offers the lifetime-employment system. Whether workers are actually persuaded to stay at the same firm for a long time is another matter. There must be a reason that makes a long-term work commitment a rational proposition. Under the seniority-based wage system young workers tend to be underpaid and older workers overpaid, relative to their productiveness. During the early years of employment the firm accumulates debts vis-à-vis the younger workers, and repays the debts with a premium when they are older. From the standpoint of workers, seniority in the firm is a nontransferable asset whose value keeps increasing over time, provided that they stay with the same firm. If they move to another firm, the asset will lose much of its value. Thus, it becomes economically rational for them to comply with the norm of the lifetime-employment system.

The seniority-based wage system exemplifies how the principles of human capitalism must be modified to suit the requirements of a particular culture. The ethos of egalitarianism is at the heart of human capitalism. Yet still strong in Japanese cultural tradition is the sense of an age-based hierarchy. The Japanese are culturally conditioned to view other people as their seniors (those above), cohorts (equals), or juniors (those below) in terms of age differences. One extreme example of Japanese consciousness of the age-based ranking hierarchy is a custom known as the *yutai* (courageous retirement) system in the ministries of the Japanese government. When a bureaucrat is promoted to the position of vice-minister in administration, the highest rank career bureaucrats can reach, the rest of his cohorts, i.e., those who entered the ministry in the same year, will all retire because a senior can lead only juniors and not his equals.

The seniority-based wage system is an attempt to reconcile the ethos of egalitarianism with the Japanese age consciousness. The fact that wages go up with seniority (the absence of jump promotion) gives workers a sense of equal treatment. At the same time the system fulfills the cultural expectation that workers within the firm should be vertically ranked by their age or the length of their tenure at the firm.

If seniority meant power, the system predictably could cause a gross misallocation of human resources, as the incompetent with more seniority would not only earn more but also have more authority in decision making than the competent with less seniority. The system avoids this trap by subtly separating seniority from power. More seniority does not necessarily imply more power. The firm in effect operates with two organization charts, nominal and real. The incompetent with high seniority may be assigned to appropriately high-ranking positions that actually do not have much power, whereas the competent with low seniority, holding apparently low-ranking posts, often are given much responsibility and power of decision making. That is why one cannot easily determine by merely looking at the formal organization chart of a Japanese firm who are the key players in the game.

The Role of the Union

Together with the lifetime-employment system and seniority-based wages, the enterprise union is commonly cited as one of the core elements of JSMS. As we saw in Chapter 2, though it bears the name "union," its role is considerably different from that of an industrial or craft union found in the capitalistic countries of the West. It is an integral component of JSMS instead of an external organization representing conflicting interest vis-à-vis management (Table XI in Appendix).

Its officers are all employees of the firm, not professional labor specialists brought in from outside. During their tenure they are paid by the union but typically retain employee status with the firm. Union fees are collected from the members, and a part of the revenue is contributed to a national federation of labor to which it belongs, in contrast to the scene in America, where the centralized industrial union first collects fees from members scattered at different firms within the industry and then distributes them back to local units. The enterprise union is financially independent, and while it maintains contact with other enterprise unions at related firms, its decision making is completely autonomous and decentralized at the firm level. It holds only a formal affiliation with the national labor organization.

Aside from collective bargaining, a majority of the firms under JSMS maintain a "mutual consultation system" whereby management and the union regularly meet and discuss the full range of topics of mutual concern. There is usually an implicit agreement that those topics being discussed under the mutual consultation system will not be taken up in collective bargaining (Table XII in Appendix).

Both in Japan and abroad the enterprise union has been criticized by many. Some argue that its pervasiveness represents the backwardness of the labor movement in Japan. Others hold that the enterprise union is essentially a form of company union, and that it is powerless, overly decentralized and localized, and subservient to management. These critiques make sense only as long as one sees the picture through the looking glass of leftist ideology or strictly from the perspective of the Western model of labor movement to which the rest of the world is expected to aspire.

If we take the position that labor will be exploited by capital as long as the nation's economy is not socialistic, then the workers under JSMS are necessarily an exploited lot. Through this looking glass the image of a "cooperative" enterprise union is transformed into a sign of docility and subservience. Such a view is hard to swallow, however, since "capitalists" in the Marxian sense are absent from the humanistic firm.

The word *modern* carries a magic connotation; it suggests something rational, desirable, advanced. Thus "modern" labor movements are to be welcomed and promoted. And it is often held that the degree of modernity of labor movements is highest in the Western capitalistic countries. As a matter of fact, however, the modernity in question means powerful union, paralyzing strikes, hostility between management and labor, excessively high wages relative to labor productivity, stifling work rules, industrial civil war. It is arguable whether these represent rationality and the advancement of industrial relations.

From the perspective of the Western model of labor movements, the enterprise union in Japan indeed seems to exemplify the underdevelopment of industrial relations. If, on the other hand, we take the premise that JSMS operates under neither socialism nor capitalism but under a new kind of economic system identified as human capitalism, the enterprise union ceases to be a puzzle or anomaly in the eye of the beholder. It flourishes because of its rationality and consistency with the expectations of the humanistic enterprise system. It is popular because its philosophy and principles are supported by the majority of workers under JSMS.

Past, Present, and Future

The accelerated growth of the Japanese economy began in the mid–1950s and continued through 1973, the year of the first oil crisis. During the same period JSMS evolved and became an identifiable, well-established framework of management within which the majority of the large firms in the leading sectors of the economy operated. JSMS was a rational system consistent with the requirements of that particular period of rapid growth, and was no doubt a significant contributing factor in the nation's economic transformation. At the same time economic growth itself helped sustain the life of JSMS.

The continually rapid growth of the economy enabled firms to actually practice the lifetime-employment system and minimum-layoff policy. Thanks to the fast economic expansion the firms' output and the number of jobs, including senior positions, kept increasing. Hence the firms could duly promote competent workers to higher posts instead of locking them in dead-end positions. During the period of accelerated growth "recession" meant a slowdown of the economy from the annual growth rate of ten percent to, say, four percent. Layoffs, therefore, were minimal in fact, and minimum-layoff policy was a reality rather than merely a propagated objective of the firms.

The firms under JSMS, in general, were engaged in large-scale manufacturing within vertically integrated industries, each maintaining a fairly high degree of autonomy in lieu of a close horizontal networking in technology and personnel with other industries. In this setting the internalized labor market, a dominant feature of JSMS, did not become a contradiction or a bottleneck to industrial growth. As each firm's output grew, so did the lifetime commitment to its prosperity of a well-integrated, cooperative, and highly motivated work force.

The oil crisis of 1973–74 was a turning point in Japan's postwar economic history. The period of ten-percent annual growth ended. The economy was beset by a severe stagflation in 1974. After the crisis the economy found itself in a new era of permanently slower growth of four to five percent per annum (Table XIII in Appendix). The oil crisis also provided a test of the viability of JSMS: whether it was in fact a system so fragile that it would collapse once the rapid economic growth stopped. An adaptation of human capitalism, JSMS demonstrated its resiliency by withstanding the shock of the depression. It did not disintegrate amid the oil crisis. The firms under JSMS did not lay off masses of workers in the name of saving themselves from bankruptcy.

From the mid–1970s to the present the Japanese economy has been experiencing repeated tidal waves of transformation. The domestic industrial structure has rapidly been shifting away from the traditional heavy and chemical industries on which the accelerated growth was founded, being replaced by the new, information-intensive industries. The economy has been increasingly internationalized. Conventional liberalization of trade and capital has been followed by the direct opening of the domestic money market and banking system to foreign interests. There has been a tremendous globalization of business, with Japanese firms shifting their production sites to overseas locations and foreign firms directly investing in Japan. Steep revaluation of the yen has been compelling the Japanese firms to redesign their strategic planning.

These far-reaching changes necessarily render aspects of "traditional" JSMS obsolete. For instance, the lifetime-employment system that guarantees workers employment at the same firm for life may be sustainable as long as the economy—and hence the firm's output—keeps expanding rapidly. But it becomes increasingly inflexible and irrational in an era of slower growth, as the firm is obliged to retain a large number of underutilized and overcompensated workers. Similarly, when market demand is highly diversified and shifting rather than simple and stable, requiring the firm to acquire new and different talents not readily available from within itself, the tightly internalized labor market becomes an obstacle to necessary external recruiting. The seniority-based wage system also turns into an irrational scheme of compensation in an age of strong demand for diverse talents. Further, consensual and participatory decision-making may prevent management from making strategic decisions with sufficient rapidity, as called for by fluid market conditions.

Japanese society itself has been changing. Greater affluence is accompanied by rising expectations. When sheer survival is the issue, one will accept any job. When one's income is modest, employment security matters a good deal. In a time of high income and opulence people, especially the capable, become more demanding. The job must be not just high paying but satisfying.

Reflecting the rise of Japanese affluence, those who change jobs in midcareer have been increasing in number. They are commonly talented middle-level managers dissatisfied with their present jobs and work environment. In order to avoid the potentially high cost of moving to another Japanese firm, they often move to foreign firms in Japan, which offer significantly higher salaries as an incentive to attract native talents. They are still a small minority, however, because moving to a foreign firm itself bears a risk. Given the future uncertainty of foreign firms in Japan, as compared to the well-established Japanese firms, the move may maximize short-term, but not necessarily their lifetime, income.

Caught by the economic and social changes in Japan, JSMS has already been changing visibly, relative to what it was like in the 1960s. Many leading firms today explicitly follow a policy of external recruiting if needed talents are not available or cannot be trained quickly enough within the firm. The trend is toward less emphasis on lifetime employment and seniority-based wages. While the basic framework of JSMS remains intact, the system is being made more flexible to meet the requirements of the new economic environment.

The trend, however, is not toward American-style management, but rather is consistent with the principles of human capitalism. Changes and adjustments of JSMS are made, typically, in the context of consensual decision making instead of unilaterally by management. For instance, as a result of chronic depression of demand for steel, the New Japan Steel has had to curtail its staff drastically and to transfer a large number of workers to newly established smaller firms in high technology as part of its product-diversification strategy. In the spirit of burden sharing, however, those fortunate enough to remain in the familiar territory of the steel business agreed to substantially replace seniority with performance as criterion for promotion.

JSMS emerged as an adaptation of human capitalism in postwar Japan. It served well in a time of accelerated growth because it was a rational and consistent system in the context of the period. More recently, major changes in the Japanese economy and society have made aspects of the system irrational, and the system has been changing in response to the dictates of the new age. In the not distant future it may bear little resemblance to what we now call JSMS. However, there is little sign that human capitalism itself is waning. The idea of people-orientation and sharing is as strongly upheld as ever. Particular rules of the new Japanese management system that emerge in the future may vary from those of traditional JSMS. But in all probability the new system, like the old, will be solidly based on the humanistic approach to management of the firm.

7

BROADER IMPLICATIONS

❏

The Making of an Egalitarian Society

By such standard criteria as distribution of income, salary gaps between top executives and production workers, and vertical occupational mobility, Japan today is among the most egalitarian industrial societies in the world (Table VIII in Appendix). Her egalitarianism, however, is a very recent phenomenon closely tied to the rise of human capitalism after World War II.

Prewar Japan, while wearing the attire of modernity, was a hierarchical and closed society relative to postwar Japan. The rigid social class structure of the feudal era was no more, but the aristocracy remained and there were new economic classes of haves and have-nots. About half of the total population lived in the rural districts, most of them poor tenant farmers. The urban masses worked in sweatshops and grease-filled factories. The layer of the middle class was thin. There was a class of rich capitalists, epitomized by the *zaibatsu* families, who reigned over major industries. There were visible signs of class distinction in terms of living style, housing, neighborhood, foods eaten, clothes worn.

The president of a family-owned firm often would claim fifty percent, or more, of the total bonuses paid out. Top executive salaries were commonly one hundred times as high as the lowest wages. There was a rigid distinction between white- and blue-collar workers, and the line was seldom crossed. White-collar workers earned salaries and some bonuses, whereas blue-collar workers received hourly wages, few or no bonuses, and, as a rule, no systematic pension benefits. Not infrequently labor was abused by powerful management.

These pictures of prewar Japan are in stark contrast to those of the nation today. At present ninety percent of the people today consider themselves middle class (Table IX in Appendix). Rich capitalists as a class have disappeared. Many of the richest people in the nation, whose list the tax authorities kindly publicize each year, are landowners and popular entertainers rather than corporate executives. A fifty-year-old senior manager's after-tax salary would probably be about three times higher than that of the newly hired worker.

A visitor to the representative humanistic firm will observe ubiquitous signs of egalitarianism. There is no separate dining room, toilet, or parking space reserved for executives. Plant managers walk around shop floors wearing a work uniform indistinguishable from that worn by regular production workers. The traditional distinction between white- and blue-collar workers has in fact vanished. Adjusted for years of schooling and service at the firm, salary differences between the two are modest. Many firms have a personnel policy such that, on the basis of demonstrated talent and ability, a production worker can be promoted to be a plant manager.

YKK, a leading Japanese manufacturer of fasteners and aluminum products, is noted for its no-nonsense egalitarianism practiced in Japan and abroad. For instance, when crates containing machines and equipment are delivered to its factory, the president, senior supervisors, or anyone else would routinely come out to unpack them. When the company built its production facilities in Macon, Georgia, a newly arrived Japanese executive flabbergasted American workers as he proceeded to clean toilets in the plant.

A society shapes, and is shaped by, the type of enterprise system that prevails within it. We perceive Soviet society as closely linked to socialism; similarly, there is a close connection between American society and capitalism. The U.S. occupation policy transformed Japan into a freer society with more equal opportunities for all than in the past. The new society, however, did not witness the rise of an American-style capitalism.

In the past centuries there were kings with divine rights, absolute monarchs, feudal lords, and emperors, who controlled vast lands and held enormous power over their peasants, serfs, and subjects. Their overwhelming rights and authority, totally unacceptable today, were viewed in their time as the natural order. In the modern age the concept of people's sovereignty has emerged, and we witness the coming of democratic nation-states that, to varying degrees, represent the people's interest. The natural order of the new era holds that people choose those by whom they are governed, instead of being ruled by someone who unilaterally and arbitrarily assumes power.

At the same time capitalism, which replaced feudalism as capital became a more important factor of production than land, retained the "feudalistic" assumption that those who own capital have the right to totally control the means of production, an assumption that continues to this day even when human resources have become as important as, or even more so than, capital. The rise of human capitalism, in a way, is analogous to the birth of a democratic modern state overcoming the irrationality of the feudal order. From the perspective of human capitalism conventional capitalism that allows a few capitalists to decide on the fate of a large corporation without the consent of numerous people who actually occupy the corporation strikes one as an anachronistic form of economic feudalism.

While there have been many capable corporate managers in postwar Japan, we cannot really single out individual heroes as responsible for Japan's economic successes. Rather, these successes, to a great extent, have been based on the collective energies mobilized by human capitalism. The conventional free-market economy encourages a few talented and ambitious individuals to exploit their potential fully but leaves a large majority of industrial workers in an environment that discourages their active and spontaneous involvement in their work.

In contrast human capitalism is people's capitalism, a private collectivism at the corporate level that forcefully persuades ordinary workers to exploit their small creativities and latent energies toward maximization of their joint productivity.

Human capitalism has also produced a society that is less pecuniarily oriented than the one capitalism has produced in America. Generally speaking, money in America is a significant symbol of social status and prestige. The more money you make, the more respect you command.

Contemporary Japan offers an alternative society, in which social prestige matters as much as pecuniary income. One's total satisfaction or sense of achievement is a function of pecuniary income and psychic income (derived from social prestige), two variables that do not necessarily go up and down together. Salaries of executives of the humanistic firms in Japan are modest by American standards, but their positions hold tremendous social prestige. The president of a small company whose money income is larger than that of a senior manager of a large firm commands less social respect than the latter. It is arguable which income—pecuniary or psychic—matters more in determining society's total well-being. An executive who annually earns half a million dollars is not necessarily ten times more satisfied than a professional making fifty thousand dollars a year. Unlike money income psychic income is tax free and not subject to the law of diminishing marginal utility. At the same time one cannot buy goods and services with psychic income.

Organized Freedom

The concept of freedom is subject to different interpretations, depending on one's ideological perspective. To most Americans America is a free society, since it guarantees market freedom as well as that of press, speech, assembly, and religion, and the communist states are not free because those freedoms (taken for granted in America) are totally or largely absent in those states. On the other hand, true socialists believe that

America, a capitalistic country where labor is exploited, is not free, and only under socialism can a genuinely free society be built. Looking to the laws of the socialist states to determine the truth will be of no help; their constitutions routinely uphold freedom, democracy, and human rights, though the words may be understood differently than they are in the West.

In the tradition of Western capitalistic ideology the belief has been strongly held that a free society is synonymous with individual freedom. But this depends on what precisely is meant by freedom. The proposition is a truism if it refers to an economic society consisting solely of individual proprietors, capitalists, and entrepreneurs. But in a contemporary capitalistic economy the representative competing units are firms rather than individuals. While there are the self-employed, doctors, lawyers, independent consultants, free-lance writers, and the like who have full access to the benefits of the free market, they account for a relatively small portion of the population. For a majority of individual workers, individual freedom amounts to the freedom to choose their employers and to quit and move to another employer; in their workplace they enjoy little individual freedom, since they do not participate in managerial decision making and are obliged to conform to the work rules defined and presented by management. For those industrial workers market freedom, an integral part of free society, means that they have freedom as they move around in the external free-labor market but not while working inside the firms. The presence of free market per se does not guarantee universal and full-fledged freedom for all individuals concerned.

From the perspective of American capitalism the humanistic enterprise system gives the impression of being rather restrictive: workers pay a heavy price by moving to another firm. The capital market, too, looks unfree, as much credit moves within each enterprise group in a highly structured manner rather than through the open, external money market. The system does not provide full market freedom; hence society built on human capitalism seems to be less free than American society. This is a rather narrow interpretation of freedom, however. What the humanistic enterprise system offers is an abundance of "organized" freedom, a concept unfamiliar to traditional capitalistic thought. If market freedom means workers' freedom to move between firms, organized freedom refers to the freedom, available within the organizational framework of the humanistic firm, for workers to participate fully in managerial decision making and to define and improve their own work rules and environment. Workers in the humanistic firm have much freedom inside the firm and less freedom than their American counterparts outside it.

Market freedom and organized freedom are substitutes; one cannot have more of both simultaneously. The humanistic enterprise generates its synergy by internalizing its work force and carefully developing the pool of firm-specific skills over the long run. This is made possible by providing workers with sufficient organized freedom inside the firm in exchange for their market freedom. If workers freely quit, the humanistic firm cannot sustain its modus operandi; it will be compelled to adopt an American-style functional management system.

Each kind of freedom has advantages and disadvantages. Market freedom gives talented individuals unlimited opportunities for economic success and encourages many to exploit their potential. At the same time, in the age of large firms, market freedom leads to an impersonal, alienating work environment for many industrial workers. On the other hand, organized freedom tends to frustrate extraordinarily talented individuals who are confined to the same firm, while satisfying and motivating the majority of industrial workers. Historically, capitalism has grown, flourished, and demonstrated its dynamism within the framework of market freedom. In light of Japan's postwar economic performance we are reminded that human capitalism, based on the principles of organized freedom, offers an alternative way of building an advanced, free economy.

Enterprise Welfare

Human capitalism has implications for the issue of welfare. Every society has to deal with the problems of poverty, destitution, unemployment, old age, and illness. In traditional society, in the absence of public welfare agencies or well-developed private insurance programs, welfare costs are absorbed mainly by families, each family extending support to its less fortunate members. Under classical capitalism the state is not expected to play a major role in providing welfare; individuals are responsible for their own. Adam Smith wrote that the government should be responsible for national security against external enemies, internal law and order, adequate social capital and infrastructure in the country, protection of the most unfortunate members of society, and for nothing else. The point was that free, able-bodied individuals should not count on government to fulfill their welfare needs. This capitalistic philosophy of welfare remained prevalent until fairly recent times. In the United States and elsewhere there were no social security or state-sponsored unemployment compensation programs of any significance before the 1930s.

With the advent of modern industrialism the static structure of traditional society begins to crumble. People become increasingly mobile, and the cohesion of the family as an institution weakens. Modern society can depend less and less on family welfare. At the same time the economy is shaken by business fluctuations, periodically throwing thousands of laid-off workers on the street, victims of depressions that they did not cause. In the face of human suffering caused by market failures, classical capitalism's view on welfare begins to sound increasingly heartless. So begins the call for a welfare state.

The trouble with the welfare state in the context of a free society is that it has a built-in propensity to be self-enhancing and self-perpetuating. It assumes that individuals are free but not responsible, which encourages people to feel entitled to benefits without paying the costs. What was once a privilege is now viewed as a right. The system breeds a new social disease, welfare dependency. People demand greater welfare benefits, as if society somehow can continue to have more than it produces.

Socialism's approach to welfare issues is not necessarily more satisfactory. In the abstract socialism is an explicitly welfare-oriented economy, the state assuming full responsibility for the nation's welfare needs. Reality, however, may considerably deviate from theory. If comprehensive economic planning to produce regular output is difficult enough, no less difficult is it for the state to plan and provide welfare goods and services to meet adequately the diverse needs of numerous individuals. Besides, comprehensive state welfare is extremely costly, and requires a highly productive economy to make it affordable. Socialism is said to be a system that maximizes welfare (equity, economic justice) at the expense of efficiency. Unfortunately, without efficiency the system cannot provide sufficient goods, including welfare goods.

Human capitalism offers a new alternative, enterprise welfare, to supplement individual, family, or state welfare. The representative humanistic firm pays a good deal of attention to the welfare needs of its workers, and regularly provides them with health care, subsidized housing, low-cost home loans, cultural and educational programs, recreational facilities, and the like. One advantage of enterprise welfare, in contrast to state welfare, is that the beneficiaries are aware that it is privately financed by their own firm and do not develop unrealistic expectations for benefits that are disproportionately large relative to what they contribute to the firm.

Perhaps the most important welfare implication of human capitalism is that it helps reduce unemployment. All humanistic firms follow a minimum-layoff policy. In recession few workers are laid off, thanks to the firms' job sharing, intrafirm transfers, and organized personnel transfers within the enterprise group. In Japan the normal rate of unemployment is about 2.5 percent, and in recession it rises to slightly above 3 percent. Some hold that low unemployment in Japan is a statistical artifact, the definition of total unemployment used by the Ministry of Labor making it more difficult for people to become unemployment statistics than in America. Even using the U.S. definition, however, the Japanese rate of unemployment increases by only 1.5 or 2 percentage points. Thus, the basic picture of low unemployment does not change, and there is little doubt that the minimum-layoff policy of the humanistic firms is one of the significant contributing factors (Table X in Appendix).

Faced with falling demand, capitalistic firms in America routinely start to externalize unemployment by sending surplus workers off to the open, free labor market, where they stay unemployed and collect benefits while waiting for the next job opportunities. The textbook depicts the open labor market as an efficient mechanism to optimize the allocation of human resources. If a visitor from outer space happened to arrive on earth in a recession period, however, he would probably mistake the "market" for some sort of dump site for wasted labor.

Both the private and social costs of unemployment are extremely high. The unemployed suffer the loss of pecuniary income and self-esteem. The rate of unemployment shows a significant positive correlation with frequency of suicide, crime, illness, divorce, and other indices of human misery. The jobless may be entitled to unemployment benefits. But the state-financed unemployment-compensation program in a way is an absurd system; the government pays people for not working while there is plenty of work to be done, which is no less absurd than a farm subsidy program that pays farmers for not producing food when people are starving. In light of this we realize the significant implication of the minimum-layoff policy, standard practice under human capitalism. It contributes to the solution of the nation's welfare problems by saving the government large sums of money and reducing waste of human resources.

The Meaning of the Workplace

Conventional economics approaches work as a disutility, something involving displeasure, discomfort, and hardship, which any normal person would wish to avoid. The wage paid to a worker is interpreted as compensation to offset the disutility of the job to be performed. The more taxing the job, the higher the wage must be. Otherwise, workers will not take the job. A dangerous and physically demanding job commands a high wage. An easy, routine job correspondingly pays a low wage.

The proposition that work is a disutility, however, while true for some people, is patently untrue for others. There are individuals for whom work is a satisfying experience and even becomes life itself. Creative artists, talented musicians, successful lawyers, productive scholars, dedicated scientists, innovative engineers, ambitious politicians, driven entrepreneurs, and the like do not perceive their work as a disutility. On the contrary, without work their lives would be empty and meaningless.

Conventional economics' contention is that these individuals are a fortunate minority, and the majority of people, especially industrial workers, have the misfortune of having to put up with displeasing jobs of one kind or another. Work is viewed as something of a necessary evil in modern society. In order to produce material affluence, a lot of industrial work, no matter how unpleasant and painful it may be, has to be performed. Either we grin and bear eight hours a day, five days a week, earn high wages, and spend our earned income on cars, bicycles, homes, appliances, books, television, vacation; or we do not work, let material civilization disintegrate, and lead a life of economic underdevelopment and poverty. We cannot have it both ways.

The idea that work is a disutility has a connection with the rise of industrialism. In the premodern world artisans and craftsmen, often working for themselves, produced things of beauty and utility with their own hands and simple tools. Their workplaces were commonly their homes as well, with their families and neighbors close by. They were poor as a reflection of an age of universal poverty, but it is doubtful that in command of their own work and its intimate environment they considered their jobs a displeasure. With industrialization, on the other hand, an increasing number of people work as employees of firms, and their workplaces become separated from their homes. The firm, their new workplace, is an economic organization providing little room for communal activity. Workers are there to earn wages in exchange for their labor and are expected to fulfill their social needs elsewhere.

Industrialism developed a scheme of dividing human inputs into two categories: blue-collar workers with brawn and white-collar workers with brain. Physically taxing industrial work would be efficiently performed by blue-collar workers without their suffering acute alienation, since they are mindless beings with a lot of muscles. Perhaps this was a reasonable assumption to make in the nineteenth century, when most workers were scarcely literate.

It is said in reference to the reported decline of American industry that a certain cultural disease has been plaguing American society, causing a weakening of the work ethic. If this is true, the cultural virus in question is of a peculiarly discriminating sort, attacking only industrial workers and not the self-employed and independent professionals, who today work as hard as in the past. A more plausible explanation seems to be that the work ethic of industrial workers has loosened because of alienation brought about by the disutility of their work. But this only begs a new question: Why were American workers more disciplined in the past than today despite the fact that since the Industrial Revolution industrial work, presumably, has always been a disutility? To deal with this question we must consider the psychology of expectations.

Human satisfaction is a function of one's expectation relative to reality. The same reality—whether an environment or a set of material possessions—can make people happy or unhappy, depending on what they expect out of life.

At the bottom of human existence are the biological needs for food and shelter. Without minimum intake of food man will soon die; without adequate shelter he will have no protection against the forces threatening his survival. As society develops, however, human needs shift from the biological to the economic and social. People cultivate a desire to live, rather than merely survive, with abundant food, clothing, entertainment, and recreation. Communal and social activities become an important element of life. With still further economic advancement come material affluence and an increased emphasis on the psychological and spiritual dimensions of human need. It is no longer enough to be well fed, sheltered, clothed, and educated; one now has a sense of self-respect and a strong desire to have one's worth duly recognized by others. No longer content with passively conforming to the conventions of society, people become interested in expressing their own views and in developing their abilities to the fullest.

Compared with the nineteenth century, industrial work in the advanced economies today is physically much easier and less dangerous, thanks to the availability of sophisticated machinery. If industrial workers from the past century returned to the earth today, they would be astonished to discover how easy work has become. There is another difference, however, between now and then. Today's industrial workers are much more affluent, educated, literate, and self-respecting, and therefore demand and expect more than their past counterparts.

Despite this difference capitalism's ethos about the industrial workplace has remained almost unchanged: industrial work is necessarily a disutility but blue-collar workers have to put up with it so as to sustain the working of industrial society. There is little genuine recognition that the workers' expectations today are different from those of the past. The workers now earn higher real wages and perform less taxing jobs than before, but these are no longer fundamental issues.

The central problem is that despite their high expectations and self-esteem, workers enjoy only second-class status to management. They are merely subjects, not full citizens, of the industrial kingdom, without the right to vote on managerial affairs of the firm in which they work. It is reasonable to suspect that a major source of alienation of American workers is management's archaic notion as to the role of "blue-collar" workers in the industrial workplace in this new age, when human resources have become far more vital than in the past century.

A sharp disparity between haves and have-nots or an acute inequality in the distribution of incomes is the stuff revolutions are made of. One problematical aspect of contemporary American capitalism is overcompensation of executives. There is something almost grotesque about an executive earning $1 million annual salary along with stock options and other benefits while workers who do the hard work for the company make fifteen dollars an hour. People are different, but not that different. A top executive of a representative humanistic firm in Japan (where per capita GNP now is higher than that of the United States) doing a comparable job earns an annual salary of about $250,000. We cannot argue that $1 million a year is necessary to induce the American counterpart to perform his task. Whether or not such an exorbitant executive salary is explainable in terms of supply and demand for managerial talents in the context of American capitalism is beside the point. What is at issue is that such a blatant income disparity within the same firm is bound to have grave consequences for the firm's productivity. In any grouping of people, if certain members of the group are disproportionately more privileged than others, the less privileged will predictably be demoralized. We thus surmise that the compensation gap between executives and workers—which has been widening rather than narrowing in recent decades in the United States—is another source of alienation of American workers.

In advanced economic societies a majority of the workforce (usually about three quarters) consists of employees of firms. In terms of time spent the firm is more important than family for many of them. In terms of consciousness or degree of attention paid as part of one's daily life, the firm is likely more significant for them than their own government. In other words, the firm as an institution occupies an extremely important position in modern society, absorbing enormous amounts of time and energy from millions of men and women.

In view of this circumstance modern capitalism has developed a peculiar mode of compartmentalizing human activity. In spite of the fact that the firm is where so many people spend so much of their lives, it is viewed more or less exclusively as an economic organization. You may have emotions at home, but the moment you arrive at your firm each morning, you are expected to transform yourself into an efficient robot with a human face. Your life is divided into segments. For personal needs count on your family. For economic needs rely on the firm. For communal needs go to church or social clubs. In truth, man is a social, economic, political, and psychological being simultaneously. There is, therefore, something unnatural about the idea that the firm is only an economic organization.

Human capitalism offers an alternative industrial society, in which the representative firms are economic as well as social organizations where people compete and cooperate, share pleasures and frustrations of work, act together to solve their common problems. It has to a large extent dissolved the pervasive alienation of workers, systemic to conventional capitalism, because workers at the humanistic firm are not second-class citizens of the industrial world but coparticipants in management of their firm in a highly egalitarian work environment. They do not suffer the strain of unnaturally having to compartmentalize their lives and go through a daily metamorphosis as they report to work, because their firm is a minicommunity, an extension of life itself.

8

COMPARISON WITH
CAPITALISM AND SOCIALISM

❏

Why Is That Man Laughing?

On the occasion of the sudden and unexpected disintegration of the socialist regimes in Eastern Europe in 1989, many Americans celebrated the triumph of capitalism. Their jubilation, however, was somewhat premature.

The East Europeans revolted against the oppressive socialism imposed under Communist-party dictatorship, but their revolution does not necessarily mean their wholesale acceptance of Western-style capitalism. On the contrary, many of them remain hopeful that they can build a humane market economy though they do not know exactly how, and are skeptical that the profit-oriented private-enterprise system based on the institution of capitalist sovereignty is their ultimate answer. And there still remain socialist regimes in the world, the largest being China, where one out of four people on earth live. Further, there are numerous individuals in the West not wholly satisfied with the capitalistic way of life.

In this chapter we shall examine both capitalism and socialism, showing how human capitalism combines the virtues and avoids the problems of each.

Similarities Between Capitalism and Socialism

The average citizen of America, a representative capitalistic society, holds an image of socialism (say, the Soviet Union prior to *glasnost* and *perestroika*) as an alternative economic system that is fundamentally and radically different from capitalism. Socialism means central economic planning and denial, as a matter of principle, of profit making and market competition. Goods and services are produced in accordance with the state-designed plan. A socialistic country may be construed as one large command economy. In contrast capitalism is a decentralized free-enterprise system where private economic agents have the freedom to make decisions, and the nation's productive activities are guided by profit motive in the context of market competition.

Yet, as we move from the macro- to microlevel and take a close look at the firms, we observe that the managerial system commonly practiced by the representative capitalistic firm in America is a vertical command system. Top management engages itself in private strategic planning for the firm, and those below dutifully conform to executive orders. The representative firm in America thus may be perceived as a mini-command economy and the American economy a collection of numerous mini-command economies. A system of centralized, vertical decision making prevails under both socialism and capitalism, though in varied manners and for different purposes.

That socialism and capitalism, in practice, are variations on the common theme of command economy is not the only similarity between the two systems. Under socialism management does not represent the interests of the firm itself. Rather, it is primarily responsible for managing the firm for the purpose of meeting the production quota as set by the planning authority. Freedom and autonomy are in the hands of the state. Management of the socialistic firm merely conforms to the state's decisions. Management of the capitalistic firm, on the other hand, has the good fortune of not having to conform to the state's planning authority. That is not to say, however, that it enjoys the luxury of complete freedom and autonomy. As we saw earlier, its decisions are often subject to constraints imposed by the stockholders and the union.

Workers under the two systems, too, share certain similarities. Both the representative socialistic and capitalistic firms practice a vertical command system rather than a consensual, participatory management system. Under both systems management makes decisions, and workers passively accept and follow those decisions. Their noninvolvement is prone to cause apathy, disinterest, and a lack of self-motivation. Few workers will voluntarily and spontaneously mobilize their inner resources and creativity toward enhancement of their productivity. Although each worker's unrealized creativity may be small, the cumulative sum of thousands of workers' lost creativity can be enormous. In this fashion, both socialism and capitalism similarly waste large sums of human resources.

America is a free country. Workers can choose their jobs and companies to work for, and they have the freedom to quit if they do not like their jobs. There is a catch, however. Most American firms practice an authoritarian, vertical command system. So when a worker becomes dissatisfied with the oppressive work environment in the present company, quits, and moves to another company, chances are that the next company is another mini–command economy that fails to give him/her freedom and autonomy. The same fate likely awaits the dissatisfied worker at the third, fourth, and other companies. As far as workers' freedom goes, the difference between workers under socialism and those under capitalism is not so much that the former are unfree and the latter free as that both are unfree in different ways. Namely, without occupational freedom workers in the planned economy are stuck at the same unfree workplace most of their productive lives, whereas workers under capitalism, with plenty of occupational freedom, may hop around a lot but, wherever they go, end up in an unfree work environment.

The work environment that denies or discourages worker participation and involvement is bound to alienate workers. Both socialistic and capitalistic firms deal with the problem by "externalizing" its source rather than facing it as an internal systemic issue. Thus in a socialistic country ideological exhortation is often used. Party leaders and ideologically oriented managers urge workers to labor valiantly and devotedly toward the noble cause of building a just and affluent socialist state. The exhortation is customarily accompanied by a hint of threat that the saboteurs, the incompetent, and the apathetic will be expelled from society as enemies of the people. This may work in the short run during a national crisis such as war or a period immediately following a revolution. The recent upheaval in Eastern Europe indicates, however, that it is not reliable over the long run.

In coping with workers' alienation the capitalistic firm in America is apt to invoke the ideology of individualism. If workers become frustrated, that is their personal, individual problem. They should solve it on their own or by talking with their friends or spouses. If they have neither friends nor spouses, they can always go to priests or psychiatrists. Even if management acknowledges that the true source of workers' alienation is their lack of freedom and autonomy, adoption of a participatory management system is not a viable option, since it is not compatible with the principle of capitalist sovereignty.

While socialism and capitalism share the similar problem of workers' alienation, the origins of the problem are not the same. The difficulty with socialism stems from the fact that the socialistic firm is an economic as well as political organization, and the firm is strained to simultaneously generate both economic and political (or ideological) efficiencies that are not necessarily consistent with one another. It is the assumption of socialism that political ideology can be as effective as economic incentives to motivate workers toward maximization of the firm's productivity. The history of socialism seems to speak for itself, that it is no more than an assumption. On the other hand, capitalism assumes that the firm can efficiently operate purely as an economic organization, and it suffers from the unreality of its assumption that the firm can achieve economic efficiency while ignoring the psychology and emotions of the workers. Human capitalism is an alternative economic system that avoids these shortcomings by explicitly recognizing the firm as an economic and social—but not political—organization.

Through a Glass, Darkly

Ideology, like religious faith, is a double-edged sword. It can be a source of enlightenment and a binding force to stir and mobilize the emotions and collective energies of men and women toward a noble cause. At the same time it may become an eyeglass that gives only a contorted, tunneled image of reality, exclusively mirroring that which is consistent with the viewer's preconceptions.

The conflicting mutual images of socialism and capitalism offer an illustration. From the perspective of socialism capitalism is an inferior economic system destined to be replaced, sooner or later, by socialism. It encourages the baser aspects of man such as greed and selfishness; it perpetuates the class struggle between capitalists and workers; it is an inherently unstable system that sends the economy through turbulent motions of boom and bust, leaving behind waves of mass unemployment; it has a built-in tendency toward monopolization of industries. A series of corrective measures that have been taken in America and other capitalistic countries—antitrust and prolabor laws, social security, welfare programs, and the like—are but the system's confession of its vulnerability and internal contradictions.

Socialism dissolves the class struggle between capitalists and workers by abolishing private ownership of the means of production. All socialistic firms are publicly owned. Under socialism emerges a sane, wholesome, compassionate society in which people live and work together for the common good rather than in pursuit of selfish, private gain at the expense of their fellow men.

From the viewpoint of capitalism such a picture of a happy, egalitarian society under socialism bears little resemblance to reality. It is not even an interesting hypothesis yet to be tested; it has already been proven wrong. Starting with the Russian

Revolution seventy years ago, socialism has been practiced in many corners of the globe, and the result has been a grand failure, almost the exact opposite of its theoretical claim. Its economy chronically suffers from stagnation, low productivity, and worker demoralization. In theory the socialist state is the workers' paradise. Why, then, have the very workers in Poland, Yugoslavia, and other socialist states revolted against their regimes?

Capitalism, like any other system, may not be flawless. But history demonstrates that it is the best and most efficient system compared to the alternatives. In eighteenth-century England the Industrial Revolution began within the framework of capitalism. The mainstream of global economic development and growth since then has, by and large, occurred in the context of free-enterprise systems. Capitalism, with its awesome dynamism, is what has changed the face of the earth, bringing about the unprecedented wealth and economic well-being of millions.

Thus, each side views the other through the ideological lens, and sees more or less what it wants to see. The picture becomes bright or dark, promising or discouraging, depending on who is using which glass.

What initiates and fortifies the ideology of each system? In the case of socialism the answer has much to do with the manner in which it came into existence. The socialist revolution was a revolution by theory promoted by a group of intellectuals, though somewhat deviating from the scenario written by Karl Marx in the mid-nineteenth century. According to Marx, as capitalism grows and matures, its inner contradictions cumulate, with mounting tensions between the haves and the have-nots. Eventually, there comes a point of spontaneous popular uprising of the masses against the capitalist regime, and capitalism will destroy itself with a bang. To be consistent with this prediction the socialist revolution should have taken place in England, home of the oldest and most mature capitalism, instead of Russia, the least developed capitalist state in Europe in the early part of the twentieth century.

Socialism began as an abstract theory of economic society, and was later put into practice by a group of ardent believers. The newly emerged regime was controlled by revolutionaries of the same ideological conviction. From their perspective the one-party system is logical because only their party represents the truth, and any other parties are therefore unpardonable counterrevolutionaries. To the true believer it is not possible to admit that the system is a failure. Intellectually and emotionally, it is easier and more comforting to think that, if the system does not work, it is not the system's fault but the fault of those who man it: incompetent managers, unmotivated supervisors, narrow-minded bureaucrats, and ignorant workers.

In contrast, the rise of capitalism was spontaneous rather than artificially induced. There was no blueprint for it. Adam Smith wrote *The Wealth of Nations* after the fact, not before. Two centuries of its success are more than sufficient to fortify its ideology.

The ideology of capitalism was further strengthened after World War II as the United States emerged as a new economic, political, and military superpower. For some quarter of a century after the war the United States remained a seemingly incontestable industrial and technological giant in the world economy. No wonder, then, that the country's extraordinary economic status nurtured, globally, a habit of thought that the American way of running business and industry is the norm.

The strength of the ideology of American capitalism meant that in the sphere of economics anything un-American tended to be interpreted as strange and abnormal, if not outright wrong. While Japan's economic growth continued, the literature on the subject by Western observers grew rapidly. The reader who combs through the literature will be struck by the frequency with which words like *exotic* and *anomalous* appear in reference to the Japanese economy, implying that many things Japanese are aberrations, a deviation from the norm, that is, the "American" norm.

This, however, is a contradiction. The Japanese economy today is the second largest in the entire world, next only to the

American economy, and to call the type of economic system found behind the industrial superpower "anomalous" is comparable to, and as misguided as, a Chinese traveler in early nineteenth-century England describing in his diary the explosive rise of classical capitalism as "an interesting anomaly." Similarly, it will not be too difficult to predict which of the two enterprise systems an extraterrestrial visitor, unfamiliar with the conflicting economic ideologies on the planet Earth, will judge "exotic": System A, under which the firm, the unit of production and competition, comprises management and workers who assume a hostile, confrontational stance against each other; or System B, under which the firm consists of management and workers closely cooperating with one another.

The eyeglass of the socialist ideology has not been of much help, either, in perceiving the reality of human capitalism. The literature on Japan's economy written by leftist observers has been variations on the theme that the impressive dedication of Japanese employees to their work represents a new, subtle form of capital's exploitation of labor, though the presence of capitalists has been obscured by the institutional trick of mutual corporate shareholding.

Each economic system develops its own frame of reference. When the point of view of one system is mechanically applied to the assessment of another system, however, the result will likely be more distorting than clarifying. Neither the capitalist nor socialist eyeglass is suited for perceiving the substance of human capitalism.

In the eighteenth century, the age of scarce capital and abundant labor, the idea of incorporation was invented and quickly became popular. Many ambitious business ventures (such as the East India Company) were highly risky and required such large sums of capital that not enough could realistically be raised from a few individual investors. The difficulty in financing big projects led to the development of the new institution of joint stock company that manages to assemble large amounts of capital by issuing and selling many shares of stock to a large number of investors. It was an ingenious idea, and its rationality and consistency with the resource constraints of the time account for the wide subsequent spread of the incorporated form of business.

Today we live in the age of abundant capital and scarce human resources. Human capitalism may be understood as a kind of human incorporation in lieu of pecuniary incorporation. It is simply an alternative way—in accord with the requirements of the new age—of organizing the firm around its human capital, rather than letting pecuniary capital be the primary basis for determining the cohesion of the corporate entity. It is no stranger, or less rational, than the idea of capital-based incorporation of business that made its appearance in the eighteenth century.

The Distribution of Power

Socialism starts with a premise that the major element of irrationality in capitalism is inordinate power given to one class of people, the capitalists, who make up only a small minority of the total population. Any economic system under which power is concentrated in the hands of a few will invite trouble because the skewed distribution of power implies that the majority are powerless, and the powerless are apt to be alienated and demoralized. One would not expect a high degree of motivation out of frustrated souls.

Socialism proceeds to solve the problem by abolishing the capitalist class and the private-property rights over the means of production. Under socialism the workers collectively own all the means of production, hence economic power is widely diffused among them. But this is pure fiction. It is not practicable for each worker to own every piece of equipment and machinery. Only conceptually does the public ownership of the means of production make sense. If all workers simultaneously try to regulate the use of their machines and tools as they see fit, the mode of production will be in a perpetual state of chaos. In practice, therefore, the state, or a small minority of the population in control of the state, takes over the task of managing the nation's economy. Since the state represents the workers' interest, this will not contradict the principle of collective ownership of the means of production.

We thus realize that socialism, in fact, inherits from capitalism the same problem that socialism is supposed to solve—concentration of power in the hands of a few. In place of the capitalists the state assumes disproportionate power. The distinction between private versus public capital is moot, inasmuch as the nation's capital is to be controlled by someone, and the inherent danger of the concentration of power is independent of whether capital controlled by some group is private or public. While it is true that the state, unlike capitalists, is not after private profit maximization, history has yet to discover outstanding exceptions to Lord Acton's dictum "Power corrupts and absolute power corrupts absolutely." It is almost a truism that the powerful privatize the benefits of their prerogatives and reserve the right to evade the responsibility presumably commensurate with their power, as witnessed by the common sight of limousines, dachas, and best seats at the Bolshoi ballet occupied by members of the upper echelon of the Soviet Communist party and their families.

Ironies and Paradoxes

Capitalism has been called a free-enterprise system because it is an economic system that firmly believes in the virtue of freedom as its fundamental, underlying value. *Freedom* is one of those magic, emotive words so often used and discussed that before long it becomes a reflex of the user's mind. Thus, to most of us the proposition that freedom is good sounds as self-evident as its corollary that anything unfree is necessarily bad.

Freedom, however, is an abstract concept, filled with ambiguity, subject to conflicting interpretations. If freedom is good, it follows that more freedom is better, and absolute freedom is best. But such a conclusion is absurd when applied to the activity of humans as social beings. We live in a community of men and women, and whatever choice we make will, favorably or adversely, affect the welfare of other members of the community. If we all are absolutely free to do anything (including murdering, maiming, deceiving, and plundering other human beings), utter chaos and anarchy will prevail; we become unfree as a consequence of too much freedom. Modifying the proposition to "Freedom is good as long as it will not harm others" will not necessarily dissolve the dilemma. In light of this new proposition with a qualifier, we are led to infer that free competition is bad since those who lose competition and go bankrupt must suffer. Furthermore, in the process of free competition the efficient win and the inefficient lose; in the end the most efficient will be the only and last survivor left in the market. The system of free competition, if unchecked, leads to the rise of monopoly and the disappearance of free competition.

Paradoxical though it may sound, sometimes freedom is achieved only by properly restricting it. For example, without being sufficiently educated first, nobody becomes a genuinely free person capable of thinking, reasoning, analyzing, and judging rationally and autonomously. Yet, education for most pupils is a long, tedious process involving many years of schooling that deprives children of much freedom to indulge in many other easier and more pleasurable activities. Similarly, it is only after years of grinding and patient practice at the keyboard at the expense of much freedom to do something else that a student of the piano attains a high degree of freedom of artistic expression.

For reasons already discussed, from the perspective of the capitalistic firm the humanistic enterprise system gives the impression of being "unfree." But what the performance of the humanistic system suggests is that economic freedom per se does not automatically and necessarily lead to efficiency, and the conventional wisdom that the freer the better is untrue. In order to build a highly integrated, productive work force, the labor market must be sufficiently internalized, meaning that the freedom of interfirm mobility need be sacrificed. For the purpose of optimizing the synergy of the firm, the consensual management system is adopted, implying that management does not have the highest degree of freedom in making its decisions. In other words, economic freedom may have positive or negative consequences on the firm's efficiency, and the precise nature of the relationship between the two is contextually determined.

Suppose that the management of a capitalistic firm desires to have the highest degree of freedom to make decisions. It wants to have the freedom to lay off surplus labor because, business being what it is, it is irrational for the firm to retain redundant workers. Management wishes to reserve the right to define work standards as it sees fit and to keep work rules as flexible as possible in the name of managerial efficiency. From labor's perspective, however, such efficiency is to be attained only at the expense of workers' freedom to determine their own work environment. They detest the idea of having to do, like slaves, exactly as told by management. Workers, being human, start to resist management's encroachment on their freedom by organizing a union and collectively demanding an ever-increasing number of inflexible work rules and rigidly defined job categories in their defense. Ironically, management's attempt to maximize the degree of freedom of managerial decision making will result in the reduction of that freedom.

It is misleading to characterize as irrational the union's unending demand for more inflexible work rules. Workers receive job-specific fixed wages, and therefore their interest will be served through maximizing wage surplus—that is, the difference between the utility of a fixed wage and the disutility of work efforts associated with the job. Since the wage is fixed irrespective of the level of work efforts, the logical way to increase wage surplus is to reduce work efforts as much as possible. If workers conform to management's wish by accepting frequent job rotations and reassignments that call for learning different skills, they must increase their work efforts and hence decrease their wage surplus. Their interest will be better served under a system of inflexible work rules and rigid job categories that eliminate the need to expend extra effort.

Efficiency and Equity

Conventional economics holds the view that while capitalism, based on the principles of free-market competition, promotes efficiency at the expense of equity, socialism, a system of economic planning, enhances equity at the cost of efficiency, the implication being that there is a trade-off between the two. Economic society cannot maximize both ends at once but has to settle for some submaximal mix of the two.

After the Great Depression of the 1930s, which gave the death blow to the classical doctrine of laissez-faire, the United States and other Western capitalistic countries proceeded to build a mixed economy, primarily a private-enterprise system mixed with a significantly large public sector that provides equity through a series of social entitlement programs such as unemployment compensation, public health insurance, public housing, and welfare. The public sector finances its programs with tax revenue collected from the private sector; it is viewed as something of a necessary evil, draining the nation's scarce resources away from the private sector, where efficiency reigns. Given the absence of competition, the public sector is necessarily inefficient; yet its presence is justified as the source of sufficient equity expected of modern society.

Anyone who reads through the conventional economic literature will be struck by the frequency with which the word *efficiency* appears. But rarely is the question "What is efficiency for?" raised for critical examination. There is a set of meanings attached to the concept of efficiency in economics, and the adequacy of the set is more or less taken for granted. Thus for the economy as a whole efficiency means the optimum allocation of the nation's limited resources, i.e., the efficient economy is one that minimizes waste in the use of its resources. For business firms efficiency means maximizing profit, the difference between total revenue and total cost.

In other words, at the level of the firms that collectively produce the nation's output, *efficiency* refers to efficiency in making money. The issue of efficiency in promoting the well-being of those who produce the output or of the relationship between efficiency in making money and that in producing worker satisfaction is usually kept aside, and is raised only if and when it has bearing on the question of the firm's profitability. Other things being equal, minimization of total cost (including labor cost) leads to a greater profit, the index of the firm's efficiency. Therefore, reducing wages as much as possible is an imperative for management concerned with the firm's efficiency, though such imperative is in serious conflict with the workers' interest. We thus realize that there may be a trade-off between efficiencies for different ends.

A similar problem appears as an ambiguity in standard economic statistics. National income is the sum of all factor incomes such as wages and salaries, rent, net interest, pretax corporate profits, incomes of unincorporated businesses. Along with gross national product, national income is often referred to as a measurement of the nation's economic well-being. Since it includes wages, higher wages will increase the size of national income, which gives the impression that the nation has become better off. However, as we turn to the standard profit-and-loss statements for the firms, the same higher wages imply less profit or more loss. The initiated and uninitiated alike will be confused as to how to put the two together; it does not seem to make sense that what's bad for business is good for the nation's economy.

Socialism is said to be an economic system that promotes equity at the expense of efficiency. As a matter of principle it negates market competition and the institution of private profit-making. Market competition being the time-tested way of promoting efficiency in producing goods and services, the fact that socialism is weak on the side of materialistic efficiency is tacitly acknowledged. As a matter of its philosophy, however, socialism holds that equity matters more than materialistic efficiency. More equity with less efficiency is preferable to more efficiency with less equity.

While such a theoretical claim is immensely appealing to many, the seventy-year history of socialism indicates that it is a claim difficult to realize in reality. The absence of market competition and economic incentives does result in critical inefficiency of the economy. The political elite in control of the state also becomes the economic elite, privatizing the use of many public goods at the expense of the masses, whose interest the state is expected to serve. Socialism does not necessarily equalize the distribution of income and wealth. Equity is not independent of efficiency, and suffers from the systemic loss of efficiency. There must be a sufficiently large pie before we can meaningfully speak of the fair sharing of it. An equitable share of little wealth is nil.

Capitalism is built on the doctrine of competition in the name of efficiency, whereas socialism advocates cooperation for the sake of equity. Conventional economics views competition and cooperation as mutually exclusive as far as enterprise systems are concerned. The firms either compete against one another or mutually cooperate. Private interfirm cooperation means private monopoly, which results in inefficiency. Public interfirm cooperation is socialism, with the same negative consequence.

Under human capitalism, in contrast, the rules of the game are arranged differently. Human capitalism is basically a free, private market economy like traditional capitalism. Keen competition persists between firms and between enterprise groups, which assures and promotes efficiency. A high degree of cooperation exists within each firm and each enterprise group. Under the system of sharing, the value added by the firm is equitably shared among its members. Under the umbrella of mutual assistance the firm, as member of the enterprise group, escapes the harsh punishment of market discipline in case of failure. Human capitalism as an institutional innovation preserves and combines the positive aspects of capitalism and socialism while resolving the systemic dilemma of the two systems so that it can simultaneously promote efficiency and equity. In this sense human capitalism may be considered the synthesis of capitalism and socialism.

9

PREVIOUS ATTEMPTS
TO REFORM
SOCIALISM AND CAPITALISM

❑

Misguided Reforms

There has been a recognition of flaws with socialism in the Eastern bloc of nations, leading to various economic reforms. The results have not been satisfactory, however, because, from the perspective of human capitalism, the reforms are misguided in one way or another, and do not strike the root causes of the problems.

After the momentous developments in Eastern Europe in 1989, China and the Soviet Union, the two giants of the Eastern bloc, today stand in contrasting positions. To overcome the stagnation of its economy China will no doubt continue to experiment with liberalization measures, as in the past, while retaining the rigid basic structure of controlled economy under the Communist-party dictatorship. Those measures will face a host of difficulties, because market competition and economic control are mutually incompatible.

The Soviet Union, on the other hand, is now trying to transform itself into an open, liberal market economy without sacrificing communitarian values. Recently Mikhail Gorbachev remarked, ''The Market is not antisocialism. It is a great invention of man.'' That is an astute observation. In June 1990 he announced that bread and meat subsidies would soon end (meaning their prices will skyrocket). The announcement touched off a massive panic buying of not only bread and meat but also all other goods to be hoarded before the anticipated inflation. The stores in the Soviet Union were emptied out. This illustrates the sort of problems his country is up against.

The communist regimes in Poland, Hungary, and Czecho-slovakia suddenly wilted away in 1989. For decades these countries had lived under centralist socialism, which in practice meant the absence of profit motives, lack of market discipline, extensive subsidies for basic commodities and services, employment security irrespective of work efforts and labor productivity, and suppressed inflation under the system of economic control. These countries are presently pleased with their newly gained freedom and political democracy. But a difficult road lies ahead. If they invoke the cold-turkey method of pursuing economic liberalization fast and on all fronts, it is bound to bring about runaway inflation, mass unemployment, and a major dislocation of the economy. If, instead, they choose a gradual approach, proceeding with a series of reforms at a measured pace, there will probably be a prolonged period of confusion and uncertainty with frequent shortage of goods and persistent unemployment. People may lose patience and start raising serious doubts about the virtue of the private-enterprise system.

Suppose they do succeed in adopting a Western-style market economy. It is not certain that the East Europeans will wholeheartedly welcome their return to square one, capitalism, noted for its inability to solve the problems of alienation of workers, unemployment, and inequities in the distribution of income and wealth, an economic system whose malaise socialism, at least by intent, was meant to cure.

In the West, too, there have been reforms of sorts meant to improve the quality of capitalism, and new schools of thought, each claiming its truth and wisdom. They all have one thing in common: They ignore, or do not pay sufficient attention to, the fact that having a free-market economy is not enough because the serious, systemic issues lie not in the market per se but inside the competing firms that make up the market economy.

Market Socialism

The dissatisfaction with the performance of the Soviet-style centrally planned and highly bureaucratized economy led to various experiments within the bloc of socialist states, in reforming the system toward one that is efficient as well as equitable. Perhaps the best known of such experiments is market socialism, alternatively called the "participatory" or "labor-managed economy" found in Yugoslavia. A system that combines selective elements of both socialism and capitalism in the hope of realizing the best of all possible worlds, it was formally introduced and put into practice in the early 1950s as the country broke off from the hegemony of the Soviet Union.

It is half socialism in that the principle of central economic planning is applied to certain basic industries, and all capital, available to the firms only from the state banks, is public rather than private. At the same time market competition exists among the firms operating outside the public sector; they may compete well and make profits or incur losses and go bankrupt.

Yugoslavian market socialism is a case of decentralization in the extreme. The basic unit of worker autonomy is not the firm but each division within the firm. It is workers who hold the ultimate rights to make decisions. All major strategic as well as operational decisions for the firm are to be discussed and approved or rejected by workers by vote under the rule of political democracy. Management, elected or approved by labor, serves the interest of workers, and not the other way around, its task being to implement the decisions made and submitted by labor.

Just as socialism may work perfectly in the abstract, the good performance of market socialism certainly is a theoretical possibility. It recognizes and accepts the efficiency-enhancing virtue of market competition. It negates private capital, so that there will be no private capitalists to exploit labor. The workers should be highly motivated, since they have the power to control their firm.

Market socialism performed reasonably well during the early years after its inception. Its overall record up to the present, however, cannot be described as impressive or brilliant. The Yugoslavian economy has been beset by chronic inflation, high unemployment, sluggishness in productivity gains, and discontent and low morale of workers, as witnessed by frequent strikes and even outright revolts against the state (such as in 1988 and 1989). This is a grand paradox, inasmuch as market socialism, at least on paper, looks to be the workers' paradise.

The malfunctioning of the system, to a degree, may be attributed to the particular geopolitical environment of the country. Yugoslavia is not a nation in the usual sense of the term. It is a composite of groups of people noted for their ethnic, cultural, and linguistic diversities. Economic development in different regions of the nation has been uneven. Not infrequently, age-old distrust between groups causes tension, hostility, and even violent confrontations. Such a setting, it may be argued, is not ideally suited for the genuine collective efforts of workers toward enhancement of their economic welfare. It appears, however, that the true explanation of the difficulties of market socialism lies elsewhere.

Market socialism is an instance of an attempt to modify and improve the economic system from the left. It is no surprise, then, that market socialism negates private capital, a symbol of the evil of capitalism. Solving one problem, however, may create another. That all capital is public means that it is socially (or collectively) owned, namely, no particular persons own it. While this sounds noble in the abstract, the fact remains that capital, like any other factor of production, must be allocated and used not by "society" but by some individual members of society. To those individual users capital is not their own; it is a free good, in the sense that it is supplied by the state banks and they do not have to pay for it. A sad aspect of human nature is that people are prone to waste things that are free to them. For any economic system to stay productive and viable, all scarce inputs, including capital, must be optimally allocated. By making capital public, market socialism implants in itself a tendency to indulge in the wasteful use of this vital resource.

Under market socialism there is no private capital and hence no shares of stocks in circulation, no dividends, no capital gains. Suppose the state bank lends capital to Firm A, which performs well and realizes surplus (profit). Firm A is permitted to lend its surplus as capital to Firm B and to collect interest on the credit, but not dividends. Even if Firm B succeeds in its investment project, financed by capital from Firm A, and generates a large surplus, Firm A is not entitled to receive any portion of that surplus as "capital gain." Such a scheme will assuredly reduce interfirm capital mobility and result in a suboptimal allocation of capital economywide. Instead, it encourages wasteful intrafirm use of capital. It has been observed that management tends to underdepreciate investment goods within the firm and to use capital to pay higher wages as a means of buying political peace from labor. Further, many firms suffer not from underinvestment but from inefficient overinvestment resulting from management's eager adoption of a capital-intensive mode of production, regardless of its economic rationality, as a way of mitigating intrafirm labor disputes through reduction of the work force.

Under market socialism the firm is the place where the workers are to enjoy the full taste of political democracy in expressing their opinions on how the firm should be run and in imposing their collective will on management. This, however, constitutes another inherent problem of the system, because political democracy and economic efficiency may be mutually incompatible. Management and workers are not one integrated whole. Workers decide and management caters to their wishes. Being human, workers make decisions that will benefit them but not necessarily the firm. Thus, management is presented with a growing number of restrictive rules such as a no-layoff policy, inflexible work standards, generous fringe benefits, and the like, which will reduce the firm's efficiency and managerial maneuverability.

The law of market socialism makes each division within the firm an autonomous unit of workers' collective decision making in the name of total grass-roots industrial democracy. Such an arrangement, however, is faulty from the standpoint of organizational efficiency. Each division, given its autonomy,

will decide in terms of what is most advantageous and beneficial to the division and not necessarily to the firm as a whole.
The firm as the unit of competition suffers because the autonomy of each division makes it difficult for management to formulate an effective, coherent, and coordinated strategy for the
firm.

Market socialism also stipulates that workers shall fully participate in managerial decision making. The letter of the law,
however, does not guarantee that they will actually do so. For
a workers' cooperative consisting of ten people total participation is a sensible approach. For a large firm with ten thousand workers it is a highly impracticable proposition. One
cannot expect ten thousand workers of a large firm to be actively involved, as stipulated by the law, in formal discussions,
analyses, and deliberations on issues of concern to the firm and
after careful thought to cast votes from a managerial perspective. It has been noted that a majority of workers under market
socialism are disinterested in active participation in management of the firm, are indifferent to the elaborate provisions of
the law guaranteeing their rights, and tend to select their managers for political, rather than economic, considerations.

The history of economic systems indicates that the concentration of economic power in one group invites trouble and
hinders the efficiency of the system. Too much power in the
hands of capitalists demoralizes workers. Socialism suffers
from the same problem because the state assumes too much
power. A powerful labor union that has arisen to counter a
powerful management will likely reduce the productive efficiency of the firm.

Those who hold power show an admirably uniform propensity not to acknowledge their power as the source of the problem and, instead, to blame others on "moral" grounds. The
capitalists deplore workers' lack of work ethic. The union
complains about management's icy indifference to workers'
welfare and explains that their tough stand is a reaction to such
indifference. The socialist state attributes workers' low productivity to their unpardonable apathy to socialist ideals.

Power may be a sure road to self-corruption but is not a proper source of self-motivation. Rather, it is a sense of responsibility that induces self-motivation, and one does not cultivate a sense of responsibility unless one is clearly aware that no one else will absorb the cost of failure.

A systemic problem of market socialism seems to be that workers assume so much power without commensurate responsibility. They have the power to control management and the firm, but when the firm fails they are entitled to generous unemployment compensation and have the prerogative to transfer to other firms. Unlike members of the humanistic firm they pay only a modest price for the firm's failure to thrive.

Market socialism is capitalism turned upside down, with power transferred from capitalists to workers. It may similarly be said that market socialism is centralist socialism turned downside up. Market socialism identifies the concentration of power in the state as the chief problem of centralist socialism, and attempts to cure it by going to the opposite extreme. The result, ironically, is alteration of the nature of the problem and not its solution. While the power group has changed, both systems suffer from a common flaw: concentration of power in one group.

Mixing Competition with Control

Since the market economy and the planned economy are antitheses of one another, it is not easy to blend the two without facing friction and contradiction. In the market economy economic agents have the freedom to make competitive decisions concerning production, distribution, and consumption of goods and services, and the allocation of the nation's resources is guided by the forces of supply and demand. In contrast the planned economy relies on economic control, rather than the free market, to solve the nation's economic problems. A central planning authority makes presumably rational decisions on what, how, and for whom to produce, the assumption of the planned economy being that under the private market economy the distribution of goods, income, and wealth will be unjust.

Under some compelling circumstances the market economy may try to practice varying degrees of economic control. Similarly, the planned economy may decide to incorporate into itself some elements of free market. Either way, combining free competition and economic control is like mixing water with oil.

When war breaks out, the market economy commonly starts to regulate prices, consumption, investment, industrial outputs, resource allocation, and other spheres of economic activity in the name of national emergency, because that is the only way to mobilize the nation's scarce resources to meet the needs of war. Control measures that require considerable sacrifice of private wants are understood to be for the duration of the war only, and the majority of citizens usually comply with the controls for the sake of survival.

Faced with national economic crises such as runaway inflation, the market economy may invoke controls even in peacetime. Incomes policy (price/wage regulations) during the 1970s in the United States is a case in point. After the multibillion-dollar Great Society program initiated by President Johnson, the Vietnam War, the dollar devaluation, and the oil shock of 1973, the American economy was beset by double-digit inflation and, later, by stagflation, a combination of high inflation and high unemployment, against which standard macroeconomic policy was seemingly inoperative. An expansionary policy would accelerate inflation, whereas a contractionary policy would worsen recession. As a substitute for standard policy a series of incomes policies was introduced.

The trouble with price/wage controls is that no matter what kind are implemented there will be difficulties. If the guidelines set by the government are lukewarm and expected to be followed on a voluntary basis, those who comply will lose and those who do not will gain—hardly an equitable proposal. If they are mandatory and comprehensive, with heavy penalties against violators, the market economy in effect transforms itself into a planned economy, with heavy costs of efficiency loss and for administration of such a nationwide scheme. If of a mandatory and selective kind, the controls will distort relative prices and start to misallocate the nation's resources. The industries selected for control suffer from suppressed prices and hence artificially reduced profits. Resources begin to move away from the controlled industries to the unregulated sectors. In order to halt the unwanted flight of resources the government may decide to extend controls to the now unregulated sectors. But at that point resources will flee to still other unsuppressed sectors, compelling the government to keep expanding the controls until all industries become regulated.

The idea of incomes policy is that since conventional macroeconomic policy cannot stop inflation or stagflation, the government should regulate prices, and if prices are held low under regulation long enough the inflationary expectations will subside, bringing about price stability. Inflationary expectation, however, is merely one of the causes of inflation. Once the lid is lifted, prices may start to rise again. The policy touches on the symptom, not the real causes, of inflation, and therefore cannot provide a fundamental solution to the problem.

Local rent control offers another example. Rent control is typically introduced in response to a situation in which, on account of an acute housing shortage, rents become so high that many people cannot afford them. The fact that rents stay high because there are people who are able or willing to pay them is ignored. Instead, the local law regulates rent increases, which implies transfer of income from property owners to tenants. Even if this is deemed equitable, the ethicality of the action cannot alter economic laws. The way to solve the problem of housing shortages is to decrease demand for housing and increase its supply, whereas rent control accomplishes the exact opposite. Low rents, thanks to the control, increase the demand for housing. Unless the entire country is under rent control, building capital moves away from the controlled area and will be invested elsewhere. The existing rental properties deteriorate because the owners neglect upkeep whose costs cannot be recovered. The supply of housing falls, and in the long run rent control will aggravate, not solve, the housing shortage.

The mixing of market and planning is not any easier when such an attempt is made from the left. The market economy is not a cure-all. It promotes efficiency by unleashing the energies of economic agents only if it is sufficiently free and competitive. If unfree, uncompetitive, and monopolized, it will instead unleash the evil forces of man—the inherent flaw of capitalism so thoroughly expounded upon by Marx and his followers. Therefore, introducing market principles in the context of a controlled economy involves an imminent danger of failure.

The economy is an extremely complicated, interlocking mechanism consisting of numerous industries, distribution systems, marketing networks, consumption goods, investment goods, public services, technicians, engineers, farmers, and multitudes of factors of production from labor, capital, land, technology, and natural resources to parts, components, and semifinished goods. Where does one begin to liberalize the economy? Which industries should be liberalized, and why? Should only the goods markets be opened up? Or must the economic reform be applied to the resources markets as well?

There is no reliable, time-tested formula to follow for the transition. Nor is there a proven theory to predict the precise outcome of the economic reform. In the context of a socialist regime it is the politicians who make the ultimate decisions on the particulars of the reform. Their decisions will likely be ad hoc, haphazard, and inconsistent, not necessarily because they are bad economists but because the free market and economic controls do not mix well and their decisions are subject to sudden reversal, as the result of the reform is unpredictable.

Suppose the steel industry remains controlled, but the home-appliances industry is liberalized. Cheap steel is available to steel users thanks to the heavy subsidy the steel industry receives from the state. The makers of home appliances, now liberalized, raise prices while using cheap steel and thus realize large profits. These, however, are not real profits associated with a free, competitive market. They are, instead, quasi-monopoly profits realizable because the makers of home appliances are now liberalized and have access to subsidized steel, whereas the makers of other, unliberalized products do not have the same advantage. Will the state authority approve such profits? Suppose further that the firms in the liberalized sector start to lay off redundant workers in order to improve their internal efficiency. The laid-off workers either remain unemployed or must be absorbed by the state-controlled firms. Will the state, once again, tolerate such a consequence of the reform?

The communist regimes implementing economic reforms have traditionally assumed that political and economic freedoms are separable, an assumption that becomes increasingly untenable as the economy moves to higher stages of development. The desire for freedom is universal, and not to recognize this fact has been a fatal flaw of communism. Advancement of the economy means an increase in the number of educated people and, at the same time, the economy's greater dependence on literate and highly trained individuals. Freedom is something of a forbidden fruit whose taste, once experienced, shall not be easily forgotten. To the educated economic freedom without political freedom is an intolerable proposition. Suppressed desires will induce a revolt of people against the regime sooner or later, as dramatically happened in China and Eastern Europe in 1989.

Codetermination

The idea that the company belongs to the stockholders and not to its workers has long been codified in company laws of the Western capitalistic countries. Such an idea made perfect sense in the age of classical capitalism, but the notion that workers are physically present in the firm merely as a matter of contract and are not its members becomes problematical in the case of a large modern corporation with many employees. Recent decades have shown an increasing realization of this, fostering a global trend toward industrial democracy. One visible sign of this trend is "codetermination," which received much publicity in the 1970s.

In theory codetermination means that management and labor jointly determine the firm's affairs, or at least that labor more actively participates in management of the firm than has traditionally been permitted. In the 1970s it was put into practice in West Germany and Scandinavian countries as a matter of formal legal requirement. (Yugoslavian market socialism is an extreme example of codetermination.) In contrast, in the United States the principles of codetermination have been experimented with on an ad hoc basis and without rewriting the company laws, as witnessed by Douglas Fraser, former president of the UAW, serving on the board of directors of the Chrysler Corporation, and by General Motors organizing its productivity teams to include representatives of both management and labor. In Japan the idea of codetermination has been spontaneously incorporated into the working of the humanistic enterprise system.

In West Germany the institution of codetermination was legalized in 1976. According to the law the firm is required to maintain, above its board of directors, a board of supervisors whose membership is equally representative of stockholders and labor. The task of the supervisors is to oversee the broad range of company affairs, from the performance of senior managers and management-labor relations to personnel policy and the financial condition of the firm. The supervisors are empowered to dismiss all executives except the president of the company, and the board of directors is obliged to comply with supervisors' decisions. In case of a deadlock the chair of the board of supervisors, who represents the stockholders, will cast the tie-breaking vote. Thus, capitalists' ultimate control of the board is preserved.

Codetermination is an attempt to infuse the principles of political democracy into management of the firm. Therein lies the problem, inasmuch as political rationality may not coincide with economic rationality. Political democracy is a means of dissolving conflict by providing institutional rules to deal peacefully with differences between concerned parties. On many issues (such as wages, benefits, and work rules), however, opinions of management and labor are predictable. Typically, codetermination amounts to finding mutually acceptable compromises. Since the firm is an economic organization, political compromises may not result in an economically optimal solution for the firm. Industrial democracy, which codetermination is meant to promote, can go in the wrong direction. Labor may become so powerful, egotistical, and shortsighted as to be able to restrict new employment, to command unwarrantedly high wages, and to paralyze the firm's management.

From the perspective of human capitalism, what is troublesome about codetermination of the sort found in West Germany is that it leaves unsolved the fundamental systemic conflict of interest between management and labor. Reportedly there has been much tension surrounding codetermination, with capitalists complaining that their rights have been violated, management being frustrated because its task is now more complicated, and workers feeling dismayed that industrial democracy is more apparent than real.

Codetermination does not alter the traditional structure of capitalism. Management still represents capitalists' interest. Workers work for, but do not really belong to, the firm. Though workers indirectly influence management through the board of supervisors, they in fact do not directly participate in managerial decision making. Industrial democracy per se is not a panacea for labor-management problems. It can result in economic efficiency of the firm, provided that both sides share a common interest. Unless this condition is met, it will more likely hamper the firm's internal efficiency. We cannot legislate organizational unity or spontaneous cooperation if none exists in the first place. The old way is that labor externalizes its hostility toward management by going on strike. Codetermination, it may be said, is legal enforcement of the internalization of labor's hostility. An improvement, perhaps. But hostility, now disguised, still remains. No similar problem is likely to develop in the humanistic firm, because workers and management therein exercise joint sovereignty, and the firm is not overseen by a board of supervisors that is ultimately controlled by the stockholders.

The Share Economy

For the self-employed, net revenue and disposable income are identical; the two go up and down together. One might say that the self-employed earn, from and for themselves, variable wages that are adjusted for their shifting business conditions.

Most industrial workers, however, receive fixed hourly wages regardless of how well their employer firms happen to be performing. In the United States the major wage contracts last for three years. If the contract has no escalator clause, real wages will fall during the contract period in the event of unexpected inflation. If the contract wages are fully indexed to inflation, real wages will stay the same during the period. In other words, real wages are set not in light of the firms' financial conditions, but by extraneous factors that have little direct connection with the working of individual firms.

Alienation of industrial workers, unemployment, and inflation are said to be the major dilemmas of modern capitalism. These problems are not unrelated to the system of fixed wages. When demand weakens, the self-employed have an option to lower their prices in order to sustain the volume of their business—an option not available to modern corporations, since wages (and hence unit labor costs) are fixed. Demand decreases, the firm is compelled to curtail production, and the resultant surplus labor is laid off. In periods of inflation the price-wage spiral begins. Higher prices lead to new higher fixed wages, which in turn induce the next round of rising prices. Thus the system of fixed wages alienates workers who are periodically dispensed with, institutionalizes unemployment as a byproduct of recession, and makes inflation a built-in feature of the economy, since wages seldom decline.

Like any other human institutions the fixed-wage system is subject to change. One proposal for change comes from Martin Weitzman, who, in his 1984 book *The Share Economy,* presents a simple yet tightly argued case for replacing the conventional fixed-wage system with a share (variable) wage system, which in a nutshell works as follows: Management and labor negotiate and settle for a ratio (say, six to four) at which total revenue of the firm is shared between them. Sixty percent of the revenue goes to labor and is paid out as wages, and forty percent to management for overhead, capital, other expenses, and profit. As the revenue pie expands or contracts, so, proportionately, do the shares of the pie. The same is true at the margin, namely, when additional labor is hired it will produce more output and more revenue, and sixty percent of the marginal (additional) revenue goes to labor and the rest to management. To maximize its profits the firm adjusts employment of labor to the level where the marginal cost of labor equals sixty percent (rather than the full value) of the marginal revenue of labor, and forty percent of the latter is added to the firm's share of the pie. The implication is that the firm is always eager to hire more labor because it is profitable to do so.

Given the law of demand, the firm must cut the price of its product in order to increase the volume of its sales. As the firm hires more labor to produce more output to be sold at a lower price, the average and marginal revenue of labor will fall, necessitating a slight drop in the average wage of workers. Assuming that the majority of the firms in the nation are now operating under the share wage system, however, this development will be only short lasting. With the firms actively and always hiring additional labor, the level of total employment nationwide will be rising along with expanding income and spending. Through the multiplier effects, aggregate demand for output will increase so that prices and wages will move up to the initial levels. The central feature of the share economy is that the firms therein operate with a built-in tendency to expand employment and lower the prices of their products. Hence in the long run the share economy, through correction of the institutional defects of modern capitalism at the micro-level, will solve the problems of unemployment and inflation more effectively than macroeconomic policy measures of the conventional varieties.

Transition from the fixed-wage economy to the share economy can be made in different ways. Tax incentive, for example, may be used, with lower income-tax rates applied to share wages than to fixed wages, which will persuade workers to seek employment at firms that totally or substantially pay share (rather than fixed) wages. To cater to the different preferences of workers, the firm may offer a mixed-compensation package consisting of a certain fixed minimum wage plus a share wage that will vary each year depending on the size of the revenue pie, a scheme reminiscent of the semiannual bonus system of Japanese firms.

The Weitzman model is not free of problems. For one thing, it makes labor an attractive input to the firm, as opposed to capital and technology. It pays to hire more labor, so the firm rationally leans toward the labor-intensive mode of production and tends to neglect new investments in the other two areas. Such a tendency will retard gains in labor productivity, which will have adverse effects on the economy in the long run.

Second, we are not certain that labor will wholeheartedly endorse the idea of the share economy when it knows that average wages will fall, at least in the short run. This particularly applies to union members with high job security, assured by their seniority. Contrary to Weitzman's claim, they may not be convinced that in the long run all workers, including themselves, will be better off, with an economy in a continual state of growth, full employment, and price stability.

In his book Weitzman remarks that, to his knowledge, the Japanese economy is the closest approximation to his share economy that actually exists in the world today, and he finds it hard to believe that there is no connection between the fact that Japan has a share economy and her economic performance. He is right in the sense that the Japanese semiannual bonus system is a variation of his share wage system. But from the perspective of the humanistic enterprise system operating in Japan, his is not really a share economy, inasmuch as the sharing in his model is restricted to division of the revenue pie between management and labor at a mutually agreeable ratio and does not extend to labor's active participation in managerial decision making.

Apart from the systemic reforms, some examples of which we have examined in this chapter, history offers numerous instances of past attempts to build communitarian economic organizations on an ad hoc or individual basis. In the United States and elsewhere there have been firms noted for their people orientation. The ESOP (Employee Stock Ownership Plan) movement may be construed as an experiment to add a touch of sharing to corporate activity in the American context. What distinguishes the humanistic enterprise system is that in postwar Japan it evolved, built a solid foundation, and demonstrated its dynamism in a manner and to a degree never in the past witnessed anywhere else.

10

THE UNIVERSALITY
OF HUMAN CAPITALISM

❑

Continuity Between Traditional and Human Capitalism

Human capitalism can best be seen as the latest evolution of capitalism. It is not a system antithetical to traditional capitalism. On the contrary, it is a continuation of Adam Smith's dream about human potential. It has faith in market competition as the time-tested means of promoting efficiency. It embraces the idea of "capital" as that which grows, multiplies, and generates the wealth of nations. The only basic difference between the two is that human capitalism places its primary value on human resources, rather than on pecuniary capital, as the foundation of wealth creation; it holds that in today's world of advanced economies, humans are the most vital of all resources, and organizes the enterprise system accordingly.

The basic continuity between traditional and human capitalism is further illustrated by the fact that human capitalism evolved in Japan as a de facto system under the formal system of capitalism. Japan did not have to rewrite its laws extensively in order to foster the emergence of a new system. By the same token those capitalistic countries that desire to introduce and promote human capitalism need not reform their internal legal systems.

There is built-in tension between traditional capitalism and socialism, because the latter arose as a revolt against the excesses and alleged flaws of the former. Since socialism is the antithesis of capitalism, it seems that human capitalism, which is compatible with traditional capitalism, should be hostile to socialism. But this is not so. Human capitalism is a competitive communitarianism that blends, as we discussed earlier, the positive aspects of capitalism and socialism while dissolving the systemic problems of the two. It is a system approachable from the right or from the left. Indeed, it can be construed as a prototype of "capitalism with a human face," which the East European countries are now aspiring to build.

Worker Cooperatives and Incentive Management

The idea and practice of the group-oriented enterprise are nothing new. Throughout the world there have been numerous examples of people-oriented business firms that fall into two broad categories (naturally with overlapping cases): One is a group of firms commonly described as "worker cooperatives," "producer cooperatives," "labor-managed firms," and the like; and the other is a group of private companies (some of them quite large and successful) that practice full-fledged incentive management with substantial or total profit-sharing and employee ownership. In the West, however, these firms have been the exceptions, whereas in Japan human capitalism became the norm, practiced by a majority of the leading, mainstream corporations.

Cooperative-type firms are bound to be organized whenever and wherever there are people dissatisfied with the existing social and economic order. The history of worker cooperatives in America is perhaps as old as the nation's history. In the nineteenth century many cooperatives were formed as the result of the workers' struggle against their employers over wages and conditions in the workplace. Numerous cooperatives likewise were started by artisans displaced by the relentless mechanization process of modern industry. The Great Depression of the 1930s brought about mass unemployment, driving a large number of individuals to found cooperatives for their survival. The cultural revolution of the late 1960s and the early 1970s stimulated many people to experiment with nonconventional workplaces. As the old cooperatives vanish, new ones continue to emerge in reaction to the centralized, bureaucratic, authoritarian mode of industrial management.

There have been successful, large-scale worker cooperatives in the United States and elsewhere. Plywood Cooperatives and Haedads Coop (in reforestation) of Oregon/Washington are well-known American examples. The Mondragon Cooperative Federation in Spain and the Scott Bader Commonwealth in Britain have been noted for their profitability, efficiency, and cohesion. Their number, however, is relatively small. The fact of the matter is that most cooperative-type firms are small, unproductive, unprofitable, and of short longevity. In a way this is perplexing. On the face of it one would suppose that the firm owned and operated by a group of people in the spirit of harmony and cooperation will be a viable business organization. If cooperatives are good, why do so many of them fail? We may consider varied reasons and evaluate them from the perspective of the humanistic enterprise system.

Not infrequently, a worker cooperative is formed by the employees of a failing company who decide to buy the firm collectively rather than face wholesale, permanent layoffs that will result from its total closure. It is no surprise, then, that the newly created cooperative often experiences continued financial difficulties on account of the inherited adverse circumstance surrounding its formation.

We may argue that the entire system of education in America is geared toward preparing a majority of students to work for conventional employers, and very few of the nation's educational resources are invested in teaching pupils the virtue of an alternative, egalitarian work environment. Consequently, the most talented, having grown up in a materialistic society, seek employment in establishment firms, where the money is. This, however, is not a problem for the humanistic firms in Japan, since they are among the most prestigious and attract many of the country's best young people.

It is often pointed out that the worker cooperative suffers from a suboptimal scale of operation and underinvestment because it lacks access to sufficient financial resources. Banks and other financial institutions are reluctant to lend money to the cooperative, since it cannot offer enough collateral, and its future looks uncertain. At the same time the cooperative hesitates to receive an amount of credit from a financial institution due to its fierce desire for autonomy and freedom from outside influences. Thus begins and continues a vicious circle of underinvestment and inefficiency. The humanistic firms in Japan avoid this trap by developing the organized capital market and establishing therein a close affiliation with major banks as a main source of debt financing. Both debtors and creditors are established firms in the nation's economy, and together generate a cumulative cycle of active investment, productivity gains, greater profits and growth of the firms, which in turn will call for more new investments.

It may be held that the ideology of individualism and freedom in America is so strong that many people are suspicious about any form of collectivism. They thus become skeptical of the cooperatives' concern with group welfare, which seems antithetical to the American way of life. Any social institution that fails to attract sufficient, positive interest from society cannot be viable, pervasive, and well established. The validity of this argument aside, in Japan the ideology is not the issue for the humanistic firms. Their competitive communitarianism is not viewed as a case of collectivism, in the sense of socialism. Their members compete and cooperate with each other for their own interest, and to them it is irrelevant whether welfare they derive from joint work efforts should be considered individualistic or group-oriented.

It is maintained that the business of worker cooperatives is often unstable because many of them go into localized services such as bookstores, restaurants, food catering, grocery stores, and the like, where market conditions tend to be precarious and unpredictable. In contrast the humanistic firms in Japan operate in all major industries and produce goods for the national and global markets.

Worker cooperatives are said to attract a ''wrong'' kind of people, those who like communal comfort but not work discipline. Further, cooperatives allegedly tend to recruit personal friends and relatives irrespective of their business acumen and work ethic, and this personal cliquism is believed to be a common cause of their inefficiency. The humanistic firms in Japan avoid this problem by screening their prospective members with utmost care.

Industrial democracy presumably works well only in a small firm. A cooperative thus faces a seeming dilemma: as long as it remains small, it can enjoy and practice industrial democracy, but its expansion will require adoption of an authoritarian management system in order to maintain cohesion and efficiency. The dilemma, however, is not necessarily real. A large firm can practice firmwide industrial democracy by combining the principles of participation and of representational democracy, as exemplified by the aforesaid Plywood Cooperatives. It consists of many small work units, each comprising ten to twenty workers who jointly manage day-to-day affairs of their unit. Each unit periodically sends its representative to the higher council that deliberates on the overall issues. The humanistic firms in Japan resolve the same dilemma by decentralizing decision making while maintaining a ranked hierarchy of management whose authority is subject to check and balance by the enterprise union exercising its intrafirm countervailing power.

Similar to worker cooperatives, incentive-management companies (i.e., those large, private firms that fully practice sharing and participatory management) also are found throughout the world. The fact that they exist in different countries under diverse political-economic systems indicates that the concept of human capitalism is universal and can cut across cultures and national boundaries. Here are some examples.

Fletcher Jones Company is an Australian example of a large, highly profitable company with the real employee ownership plan. It began as a men's clothing store in Warrnambool in 1924, and its central office was established in Melbourne in 1928. The company had thirty-one stores and three thousand employees in 1974. Shares of the company stock with full dividend and voting rights are held by all employees; the Jones family owns thirty percent of shares, the employees seventy percent. There are no absentee stockholders, and stocks are not for sale on the stock exchange. If an employee stockholder leaves the company, the shares must be sold back to the firm. When an employee retires, the shares retain their original vesting until the employee's death; then, his or her survivors are required to sell them back to the company on inheriting them.

JZD Agrokombinát Slušovice of Czechoslovakia is a remarkable instance of an incentive-management firm that has flourished under a most rigid, centrally planned socialist regime. It fully implements the Bat'a system developed during the 1920s and '30s by Tomáš Baťa, a great Czechoslovakian entrepreneur and management expert. The system advocates decentralized organization, departmental autonomy, self-management, profit sharing, long-term employment, reinvestment of earnings, workers' total coownership of the firm, and in-house management education and training. The system considers the quality of life of its employees—encompassing workplace, health care, housing, and social services—to be primary company responsibility, and disapproves of subsidies, debts, public stocks, unions, preferential customs, or quotas. JZD initially started as a collective farm. In 1969 it began to expand and diversify under the direction of Ing F. Čuba. Today its three thousand workers produce, among other products, food, electronic computers, computer software, construction equipment, agricultural machinery, fertilizers, and top racehorses.

Lincoln Electric in Cleveland, Ohio is a notable example of a private, successful American company operating on the basis of total profit sharing and employee ownership. It is the world's largest producer of electrodes and welding machines as well as one of the highest-paying factories in the world, and is known for the highest quality and the lowest prices. The company was founded by James F. Lincoln in 1925 with a stock-purchase plan for all employees, introduced a suggestion system in 1929, and instituted the bonus plan in 1934. By 1944 there was a comprehensive pension plan, and the systems of promotion from within and of continuous employment were fully practiced. Lincoln operates basically in the same way as the representative humanistic firm in Japan.

The company believes that its growth depends on customers, who ultimately supply money needed for expansion. In this sense the customers' interest comes before the stockholders'. It also believes that financing for company expansion should come from within the firm—through initial cash investment by the founders, retained earnings, and stock purchase by those who work in the business. Workers who leave the company are required to sell their shares back to Lincoln (as at Fletcher Jones). New employees may receive a credit from the company to purchase the company stock. Lincoln does not rely on borrowing for its capital formation; debt is limited to current payables.

There has never been a formal organization chart at Lincoln. The system of supervision is kept informal and unstructured. Each worker is trained to perform multiple skills. A typical Lincoln worker earns about twice as much as the comparable factory workers in the Cleveland area. Since 1949 no layoffs have occurred at Lincoln.

In 1951 James F. Lincoln wrote a book, *Incentive Management,* in which he explained his philosophy of management. While researching for this essay I encountered his book lying dust covered in my university library. As I read it, I was astonished to discover that it is a bible of human capitalism that discusses and advocates, in simple language, the principles of sharing and joint management-worker sovereignty as the only sensible and viable way to manage the firm in an industrial society. Lincoln wrote four decades ago: "It is . . . hard to understand why companies which have been vexed by labor-management friction do not go to incentive management. How long must the country wait before it can have the benefits of such natural and obvious cooperation in industry? Such cooperation is taken for granted and is continuous in many other activities of man. It is in industry, however, where it is most needed."

We thus realize that human capitalism is hardly new. It has been with us for a long time, practiced by many firms in America and elsewhere, though they have not become the mainstream institutions outside Japan. It is a familiar concept whose universal significance and full-scale applicability have not been widely recognized or well understood.

Exporting Human Capitalism

Anything—whether art, music, literature, or social institutions—that makes sense in human terms is destined to move across national boundaries. The export of human capitalism, in fact, has already been happening. The process of its transfer abroad, however, has been filled with a good deal of confusion. Japan's economic growth produced numerous books, countless magazine articles, and voluminous mass-media reports on the subject. Many symposia, conferences, and seminars have been held on the secret of Japanese business. But most of the reporting has been a response to the rising curiosity in the outside world about the Japanese economy, without a clear focus on or vision of what has really happened to the economic system in postwar Japan. As a result the literature has touched only inadvertently on aspects of human capitalism.

To add further confusion human capitalism has not been properly distinguished from the Japanese-style management system, while the literature's assessment of JSMS has flip-flopped more than once. In the 1950s and the early 1960s many Western observers held that JSMS was probably the worst management system imaginable. Later, it received a positive appraisal. More recently, the onetime enthusiasm about the system has subsided, while JSMS itself has been changing.

On the one hand, American industry cannot really practice JSMS as such, which is a product of Japanese culture. Unless Americans migrated to the Japanese islands en masse and lived there for two thousand years, they could not possibly behave as Japanese do. At the same time Americans have been perplexed by the fact that the surveys of excellent companies and vanguard firms in America often reveal characteristics that seem to resemble those of Japanese management.

Three American authors put the matter in perspective. William G. Ouchi, in his popular book *Theory Z*, reminded us that there are excellent American companies (for example, IBM, Hewlett-Packard, Eastman Kodak, Procter & Gamble) whose managements skillfully apply the (Japanese) art of dealing with the delicate issues of trust, subtlety, and intimacy in human relations, an art that they developed on their own rather than borrowed from Japanese management. In another equally popular book, *The Art of Japanese Management,* Richard Tanner Pascale and Anthony G. Athos showed that there are American companies (such as IBM, Boeing, United Airlines, Delta Airlines, 3M) that understand as well as Japanese companies the importance of implicit and informal (as against explicit and formal) rules in coping with ambiguity, uncertainty, and the imperfection of human connections in the work environment.

Human capitalism has been reaching the United States not as part of an extensive economic reform, but rather as a predictable process accompanying Japan's economic expansion. In theory the abstract principles of human capitalism are rational and universal and hence readily transferable to other lands. In practice what attracts the attention of outside observers is the particular managerial system that operates in Japan. Inasmuch as JSMS is an adaptation of human capitalism to specific expectations of Japanese culture, many aspects of it will nonetheless strike the non-Japanese as unusual and unfamiliar. We may assume that when JSMS is exported, those aspects of it that are culture bound will be rejected or adapted to suit the new culture.

The Japanese management system has been introduced to American firms mainly in three ways. First, many American firms that are not in direct competition with the Japanese have been trying to improve their management systems on their own. With the learn-from-Japan boom a number of them have paid close attention to the Japanese practice in search of object lessons. Second, those American firms competing with the Japanese have been compelled to study the Japanese principles as a matter of strategy. Third, an increasing number of Japanese firms have been directly investing in the United States, and they transmit their methods and ideas to American managers and workers. In no cases have any of the specifically Japanese aspects of the system—such as the seniority-based wage system, the ranked hierarchy whereby higher seniority does not necessarily mean higher authority, the idea of "lifetime employment," etc.—been successfully transplanted to American soil.

Japanese firms operating in the United States are direct conveyors of human capitalism. We should, therefore, be able to learn a great deal from them about the transferability of the new economic system. There are points of caution, however. Those firms are in America to make money, and are not on a mission to teach America the doctrine of human capitalism. They are here because trade frictions between the United States and Japan on account of chronic and huge bilateral trade imbalances have made the approach of direct foreign investment more advantageous than an export strategy. They are attracted to the United States, despite their language difficulty and unfamiliarity with American customs, since the United States is a huge, rich, potentially lucrative market where land, energies, and labor have become inexpensive relative to those in Japan, thanks to steep revaluation of the yen. We must also remember that the Japanese firms in America are diverse in size, product category, character, experience, philosophy, and managerial competence. While many of them have been successful, others, especially small ones, have performed poorly or failed completely.

Japanese Automobile Companies in America

The major automobile manufacturers of Japan have been directly investing in the United States. Those companies, as they operate in Japan, are technologically advanced, managerially efficient, profitable, and represent the Japanese prototype of the humanistic enterprise. When they come to America, they carry with them their way of managing the firm, though they are not necessarily conscious that their way is "human capitalism" as such. The managers of these firms *are* aware that their way cannot be directly and literally transplanted to the United States. They know that it needs to be modified and adjusted to the requirements of American culture. They generally follow a pragmatic approach, adopting whatever works and discarding those practices that stir American workers' resistance. In other words, unwittingly they are conducting experiments in the exportability of human capitalism and the feasibility of constructing an American prototype of the humanistic enterprise. Their findings and experiences, then, should reveal much truth about the new system.

Nummi (a Toyota-GM joint venture) in California, Nissan in Tennessee, and Honda in Ohio are the leading Japanese automakers now operating in the United States under Japanese management. Their general strategy for the American market is the same, and their methods of doing business in America show common characteristics.

The main thrust of the humanistic enterprise is to build a well-integrated internal work force whose members make a long-term commitment and continually learn and develop firm-specific contextual skills. To achieve this end the Japanese automaker in America begins with a careful screening of native job applicants, who go through elaborate, multiphasic testing that includes written examinations, interviews, and performance tests. (At Nummi, UAW officers and the management jointly evaluate new job applicants.) The purpose of the screening, which looks extra cautious by American standards, is to choose physically able, mentally stable, cooperative, and inquisitive individuals and to reject antisocial, abrasive, confrontational personalities. This is a prerequisite that cannot be compromised, since the firm is not going to rely, American-style, on the external labor market, through which workers come and go without any sense of affiliation with the firm.

From among the accepted applicants a select group of workers is appointed for various leadership positions on the basis of their talent, experience, and aptitude. They are then sent to the headquarters in Japan for lengthy and thorough training in technical skills and the philosophy of harmonious, integrative, and participatory management. Upon return to the United States they, together with Japanese trainers, train American workers in the local plant. As the firm's central concern is maintenance of the highest quality of manufacturing, nothing is left to chance or wishful thinking. No one without sufficient training is permitted to work on the shop floor.

The total cost of sending a large number of American workers all the way to Japan, of bringing the Japanese technical staff to production sites in the United States for further training of Americans, and of conducting more specialized and advanced training programs in both countries on a continual basis is extremely high. But it is the cost of investing in human assets that cannot be avoided in order to build a competent, well-integrated work force.

As in Japan, the firms in America practice and promote industrial democracy. Any status symbol that ferments class consciousness is removed from the workplace. There are no parking spaces or toilets reserved for executives. Managers and workers dine in the common cafeteria. Administrative workers, including senior managers, work in the open office instead of behind closed doors. Production workers are called "associates" or "technicians" rather than "workers" or "employees."

Each firm maintains an open communication system, which enables anyone to speak to any manager to register complaints or to make suggestions for the firm. Whenever possible, problems (e.g., the need to install a water fountain or a better ventilation system) are quickly and informally dealt with on the spot rather than through a formal grievance channel. The building in Fremont, California, that Nummi now occupies used to be GM's assembly plant noted for high absenteeism, low worker morale, and rampant use of alcohol and drugs among employees during their work hours. Under GM management the number of pending grievances reached two thousand. By the terms of agreement between UAW and Toyota the majority of workers at Nummi are former employees of GM at Fremont, all belonging to the union. Despite the basic sameness of the work force the number of pending grievances under Toyota management was down to ten in 1986.

The firms deliberately avoid job specialization. The number of job categories is reduced to a handful relative to the traditional practice in the American auto companies. All production workers rotate their jobs, instead of concentrating on one particular task, in order for them to cultivate a holistic and contextual understanding of their work.

Cooperation, involvement, participation, are the key concepts constantly stressed by the Japanese firms. Technical decision making is decentralized and localized as much as possible. Workers assume responsibility not only for their jobs but also for betterment of their work standards. They are encouraged to involve themselves in "continual improvement" *(kaizen),* sharing ideas and discussing mutual problems with their associates. Anyone on the floor is authorized to stop the entire assembly line if any problem that may jeopardize the quality of products is spotted, an unprecedented practice in traditional American auto manufacturing.

As in Japan, the firms practice the minimum-layoff policy, providing workers with long-term employment security. Despite the high quality rating bestowed on them by independent testing agencies, Nummi faced sluggish demand for its models, Nova and Corolla FX, during the early phase of its operation in California. In 1986 it sold only 180,000 units instead of the targeted 250,000. This was a situation in which an American automobile company would most probably lay off a large number of its workers. Understandably, tension and apprehension began to develop among Nummi employees. But there was no layoff. Instead, surplus workers were placed on special training programs. Similarly, in the spring of 1988, Nissan in Tennessee kept its pledge of a minimum-layoff policy when it was hard hit by a sales slump. The company slowed line speed, gave workers new trainings in safety, communications, and shop-floor management, but did not lay off a single employee.

Dismissals of workers for their negligence or misconduct have been rare. A few cases that have occurred were not unilaterally executed by management but with the close consultation and approval of the associates of the dismissed. For example, at Honda in Ohio the matter is handled by a fairness committee consisting of six associates (workers) and one member representing the management.

The compensation system is one area in which some issues are still unresolved. Japanese automakers in America compensate their workers with wages and fringe benefits that are roughly comparable to those of unionized workers at the American auto manufacturing firms and usually are about forty percent higher than manufacturing wages for similar work in their localities. One problem that Japanese management faces is the equitable determination of wages. Much work is done as a team, and when members of the team rotate jobs, it is difficult to measure productivity of an individual worker. Wages are set mainly in terms of job category, but those in the same category obviously are not equally productive. Besides, how to compensate a team leader relative to members of the team is a delicate question.

In Japan the executives' market is internalized, and consequently their salaries are much lower than those of American counterparts, in accordance with enterprise egalitarianism. The Japanese automakers in America, however, can recruit experienced American auto executives only at market rates, a practice that makes the compensation gap between top and bottom wider in America than in Japan. Not enough time has passed for the Japanese firms to train and recruit senior executives from their ranks. Whether in the future the internally recruited American senior managers will be satisfied with salaries adjusted lower than market rates in the name of human capitalism is a question that remains to be answered.

One requirement of the humanistic enterprise system is that its management enjoy autonomy and freedom from outside control, so that it can pursue a long-term growth strategy instead of an unwanted policy of short-term profit maximization. This condition is met for the Japanese automakers in America, since they are wholly or substantially owned by the parent corporations in Japan and heavily rely on debt financing of large initial investment costs with credit from the affiliated Japanese banks. In the case of Nummi the joint-venture contract entitles Toyota to full management rights.

It is unrealistic to think that there can be a management system that will satisfy everyone. Some American workers have left the Japanese firms voluntarily for one reason or another. There have been isolated reports that the Japanese management method in fact is neo-Taylorism or management by stress that relentlessly pressures employees to speed up their work in the name of involvement and self-motivation.

For example, Mike Parker and Jane Slaughter, who describe themselves as former autoworkers, charged: ". . . Nummi has achieved its gains through far greater regimentation of the work force than exists in traditional American auto plants. Tight specifications and monitoring of how jobs are to be done, a bare-bones work force with no replacements for absentees and a systematic and continuing speedup are the methods used." (*The New York Times,* December 4, 1988.) To this responded Bruce Lee, director of the United Automobile Workers Western region, who was involved in the creation of the Nummi joint venture: "[N]either of these journalists has ever worked at Nummi, nor done any on-the-spot reporting there. Neither our own local union people nor local management has any record of Mr. Parker or Ms. Slaughter ever setting foot in the plant. They have never even spoken with any of the UAW people who played key roles in the creation of Nummi's team system. Their article's slant clearly reflects an unstated politi-

cal agenda. It certainly is not based on firsthand knowledge."
(*The New York Times,* December 25, 1988.)

Most American workers have not left the Japanese firms.
There has been no revolt of American associates against Japanese management. On the contrary, a majority of them have
been pleased and satisfied with their workplace. Many of them
have expressed their excitement at working in a familylike
company. Those who had previously worked for American
firms under traditional American management have been surprised to discover that the new management does care about
workers.

Diane Howard, team leader of Nummi Front Bumper Squad
Number Four, explains: "Any team member can call for a
group meeting to discuss our work—and Nummi will pay us
overtime for the discussion. I can't tell you how important that
sort of thing is, the notion that they trust us. We don't punch
in or out anymore. We don't have to get passes to go to the
medical clinic. It's made us care about the quality of these
cars. American cars were famous for their sloppy work. But
now, we have this feeling that we're in it together." She adds,
"You talk to almost anyone at Nummi and you'll hear the same
thing: Finally, someone is giving us an opportunity to be
treated with respect."

Not long ago it was commonly said that Americans are so
individualistic that they will thoroughly reject group orientation of the Japanese firms when they come to the United
States. Such conventional wisdom has proven to be largely a
myth. It seems that there has been much misperception in
America about the reality of traditional American management. Many people have thought that the coolness and impersonality of American managerialism persists in part because
that is what individualistic American workers want. The experiences of the Japanese firms in America show that in truth
many "individualistic" American workers prefer a "familylike" work environment not because they, in the course of
their preliminary training, have been indoctrinated to become

hard-core Japanophiles but rather because it makes sense in simple human terms.

/ American workers in the Japanese auto companies are the first generation of Americans directly and fully exposed to human capitalism/ They have demonstrated that the principles of human capitalism offer an acceptable and sensible alternative to those of conventional capitalism. They also have thus far rejected traditional unionism as irrelevant in this new context. The UAW has not been able to penetrate Honda in Ohio or Nissan in Tennessee. In 1986 the UAW withdrew its attempt to unionize Honda, having learned that seventy-five percent of Honda workers were against it. And in July 1989 the Nissan workers startled the nation by voting two to one against the UAW. Japanese management is not against unions; it is against an outside union that comes in and interferes with internal affairs of its firm. The UAW at Nummi in California functions as a de facto enterprise union, since the existing contract applies only to Nummi. It is noteworthy that the Honda workers in Ohio have organized the Associates' Alliance, which may later evolve into a full-fledged enterprise union. If so, it will be the first such union to emerge from the American prototype of the humanistic enterprise.

Humanizing Industrial Relations in America

There has been a growing recognition in America that the traditional system of industrial management, characterized by adversarial employer-employee relations, is counterproductive to both parties. This recognition has led to a search for alternatives to the conventional practices. In the past two decades the old system has moved toward a more "humanized" mode of industrial relations.

Darwinism operates in the market economy. Any managerial system that is not fit enough to produce high-quality products is destined for extinction, since the companies practicing it cannot survive in the marketplace. The flaws of the American system became visible in the late 1960s and the early

1970s, with the intensification of foreign competition in the American and world markets. An increasing number of American firms in a wide range of industries lost their market shares, and were thus compelled to look for a solution to the problem. The American automobile industry, in particular, faced a crisis. The industry's loss of competitive edge was matched by the abysmal demoralization of the autoworkers. There was a time when they would knowingly allow defective products to pass through stages of production or even maliciously damage the very cars they were assembling.

Another test of the viability of a managerial system is by its exportability to other countries. If the system is good, it should work at home as well as abroad. Of numerous American (and Western) firms now directly investing in Japan, the majority of the excellent companies are known to practice the basic principles of people orientation. Few of the firms that tried to introduce the traditional American-style management system have succeeded in Japan. In contrast, the reverse has been the case with Japanese transplants in America. They naturally make mistakes because of their unfamiliarity with the language, culture, laws, and social conventions of the host country, but the humanistic approach to management that most of them bring to America has been well received by the local employees.

The humanistic approach is welcomed in America because it gives the workers what they desire but have been denied under the conventional American system: industrial democracy, corporate community, and egalitarianism. It upgrades their status. The result, often, is a conspicuous change in employee attitudes—from dejection to enthusiasm, from suspicion to trust, from hostility to cooperation, from divisiveness to consensus, from jurisdictional isolation to wide-ranging participation, from passive obedience to managerial authority to active involvement.

James D. Hodgson, former secretary of labor, described such a change at Nummi when he spoke before an audience of the Industrial Relations Research Association in 1987: "What a change there is now from the shabby chaos that prevailed in the same plant with much the same work force only a few years ago when it operated under old-line American management!''

In 1979 another ''industrial miracle'' occurred at the Edison, New Jersey, plant of Ford Motor Company when management introduced an employee-participation program named EI (Employee Involvement). Its centerpiece is the ''stop-button'' system whereby workers can stop the assembly line whenever they detect quality-impairing problems—a radical step taken by an American automobile manufacturer whose founder, Henry Ford, once remarked, ''The assembly line is a haven for those who haven't got the brains to do anything else.'' The program makes everyone on the shop floor a quality controller. Worker morale rose visibly, and the number of defects per car assembled at the Edison plant dropped from seventeen to one. Subsequently EI was adopted by a majority of Ford plants in the country. From 1980 to 1984 the number of ''things gone wrong'' with Ford cars decreased by fifty-five percent.

Since the 1950s and '60s—the heyday of the American-style managerial system with militant, adversarial unions—the rate of unionization has been steadily declining, while the number of nonunion firms that are committed to employee welfare and match or outmatch unionized firms in granting to their employees what unions can obtain through collective bargaining has been increasing. In America being antiunion is no longer antisocial. Today many American workers seem to be more company oriented and skeptical about the virtue of a large industrial union than in the past. American managers, employees, and society at large are currently exploring alternative ways of organizing the systems of human resource development and industrial relations. In this search the Japanese companies have been a significant source of influence. Honda and Nissan have made a historic contribution by adding non-union auto plants to a traditionally fully unionized industry. They have shown that they work quite well in this major industry. Nummi has demonstrated that the ''internalized'' union is a viable option even in the American context. The trend appears to be away from confrontational industry- or craft-based unions and toward cooperative enterprise-based (in-house) labor organizations.

This is not sheer speculation. Canadian unions have already broken off from the UAW, and some American locals may start to follow suit in the near future. There is no legal obstacle to the process. The National Labor Relations Act defines *labor organization* as "any organization of any kind" including "employee-representation committee or plan, in which employees participate and which exists for the purpose . . . of dealing with employers concerning grievances, labor disputes, wages, rates of pay, hours of employment, or conditions of work." This definition duly covers enterprise unions of varied sorts. Of course, an in-house union can be as adversarial as an industrial union. More important than the form of labor organization is a genuine understanding that cooperative industrial management is good because it is a positive-sum game that is gainful to both management and labor. We recall that the industrial relations in Japan during the early postwar years were just as acrimonious as those in America in the 1950s. The harmonious industrial management found in present-day Japan is a product of mutual learning and efforts by management and workers. What took place in Japan certainly can happen in America.

Human Capitalism in Great Britain

Over the past decade or so the manufacturing and financial sectors of the British economy have been revitalized, to a significant degree, by a massive infusion of Japanese capital, technology, and managerial know-how. Within the next twenty years—according to a report by the Confederation of British Industry—at least fifteen percent of British industrial output could be produced by Japanese-owned companies. These companies are also expected to export products worth more than £13 billion (U.S. $20 billion) per year, sizably contributing to Britain's balance of trade.

Today a growing number of British workers and managers work at Japanese firms that transfer to Britain the new managerial method, attitude, and philosophy, replacing the old practices. The process has, arguably, been called "Japanization" of British industry. Keith Thurley, professor of industrial relations and personnel management at the London School of Economics and Political Science, comments: "Factory management in Britain has not had a high status, and the Japanese have reversed this. There is a knowledge and a capacity within management organizations which is superior to anything in Britain. It's not that Japanese organization can't go wrong, but it is capable of mobilizing a type of team approach to the solution of problems which is extremely impressive to me. It can apply to research, it can apply to product development, getting a project done on time. It is a capacity the British do have but only under crisis Dunkirk conditions."

Britain offers an interesting ground for testing the universality of human capitalism, as embodied in the Japanese management system, because British industry, like its American counterpart, has been plagued by adversarial management-labor relations, strong trade unions, and restrictive working practices and, in addition, by class conflict and status distinction of the sort that is largely absent in America. There is a wide and deep gulf separating the workers from the management side. The two groups differ in language, demeanor, lifestyles, educational backgrounds; they lead segregated lives, seldom intermingling with each other socially and personally; workers feel a sense of apartness, alienation, and antagonism against managers and engineers. Not surprisingly, the traditional work ethic has long been on the wane. All this is the exact opposite of communitarianism as represented by human capitalism.

A study of Japanese subsidiaries in manufacturing and financial services by Michael White and Malcolm Trevor reveals that Japanese management practices in Britain are essentially the same as those in America. The Japanese firms in Britain operate with long time-horizons; put a tremendous emphasis on the quality of their products; prefer a lean, informal, and flexible organizational structure; minimize status distinction; practice a minimum-layoff policy; carefully screen new employees; share with workers much information on financial conditions, business outlook, and production plans; stress the importance of harmony and cooperation, and the like. We observe that these practices are manifestations of corporate egalitarianism, and not necessarily "Japanese." Understandably, the specifically Japanese practices such as lifetime employment, seniority-based wages, and enterprise unions are conspicuously missing from the list.

According to the White/Trevor study British workers seem more impressed than their American counterparts by the egalitarian and "classless" outlook and behavior of Japanese managers (a fact that reflects the British workers' class consciousness), and they tend to be more critical of British managers than of Japanese managers. The study further shows that the British workers' reaction to the firm's mixed managerial group becomes more favorable the greater the Japanese presence and influence.

Jeremy Golden, Anglo-Japanese liaison officer with the Milton Keynes Development Corporation, explains: "I don't think the British are very good at communicating—there is something in the way we talk and the class divisions that make it difficult for us to penetrate. Even if the British manager has good intentions, the way he says things tends to be antagonistic. Very often the workers feel patronized and the manager feels his work force is being rebellious or subversive. . . . Even considering the linguistic difficulties between the Japanese manager and British worker, it is easier for them to communicate. The manager's English might not be so hot, but his spirit is with the company and with the worker. He might be putting down that worker or imposing strict tea breaks, but he is not putting down the worker's class—he doesn't give a damn about class, he cares only about the company."

A distinct aspect of Japanese management in Britain, as in America, is its working practices and operational methods on the shop floor: a meticulous attention to quality control and the details of the production process; managers' hands-on involvement; work discipline; small-group activities to enhance workers' sense of participation and cooperation. The above study reports that British workers respond positively to responsibility and discipline, recognize that work is a serious business, appreciate the fact that managers work hard and care for employees as individual human beings, and even experience a feeling of pride at being part of such an exceptional effort. They readily accept managerial authority based on technical competence and dedication to high-quality work, and not on mere status distinction.

The lesson of Japanese firms' experiences in Britain seems to be that the long-assumed demise of the work ethic in Britain probably is a myth. The secret of successful management is not the "Japanese" system, but, simply, the attitude and philosophy of management toward workers and the workplace. When Ronald Dore, a British expert on Japan, predicted in 1973 that the British industrial system would be converging to the Japanese system, the general reaction was stunned disbelief. Today, it appears that his prophecy (which should be rephrased as "convergence to human capitalism") is becoming a reality.

Prospects

The international transfer of an economic system is conditioned by the geopolitical status of the nation from which the system is to be exported. If the nation is powerful, its economic system tends to be imitated by weaker nations. The global spread of capitalism in the nineteenth century was no doubt greatly facilitated by the hegemonic power of Great Britain presiding over its far-reaching empire. Similarly, in the twentieth century a further global transfer of capitalism was promoted by the United States, the newly emerged world economic power, and the process was accelerated after World War II when the United States became the superhegemon of the century.

Japan, the exporter of human capitalism, lacks the advantages held by Great Britain and the United States in the earlier periods. The country today is an economic giant without major arms. Given the weight of the U.S. and West European economies in the world, Japan is not powerful enough to be a new world leader, comparable to Britain in the nineteenth century or to the United States in the mid-twentieth century.

Exportability of an economic system also depends on ease of communication. Japanese managers overseas suffer a linguistic handicap relative to their American counterparts, because English, the international language, is not their native tongue, whereas American managers have been able to communicate in their own language with many of their foreign colleagues.

In a way it is more difficult to transfer human capitalism abroad than traditional capitalism. The heart of human capitalism is people orientation in contrast to the money orientation of traditional capitalism. People being emotional and psychological beings, it is a far more taxing job to build a viable enterprise centered around a group of people who possess conflicting views, values, and feelings than to manage a company whose cohesion is sustained by the cool and impersonal logic of money, contract, and specialization. The problem is compounded when the people to be dealt with speak a strange tongue and breathe the air of an alien culture.

Despite these disadvantages the transfer of human capitalism from Japan to the rest of the world, in all likelihood, will continue and the process will perhaps be accelerated in the future, because the new system echoes the rising global sentiment for a more humanized workplace and industrial management than traditional capitalism or socialism has been able to offer. The twenty-first century will witness the prevalence of a people-oriented economic system in one form or another. The future practitioners of human capitalism worldwide will be attracted to the new system for its basic rationality and universally persuasive principles, and will, we may speculate, be largely oblivious of its Japanese origin, just as today's practitioners of capitalism throughout the world do not consider themselves to be transmitters of an English tradition.

Conclusion

Human capitalism is a reaffirmation of Adam Smith's wisdom, expressed over two centuries ago, that free competition in the marketplace is what makes an efficient and dynamic economy. It is also an institutional innovation to correct what's wrong with Adam Smith, who did not anticipate the coming of the large industrial corporations with the impersonal workplaces that are bound to demoralize workers, and who thus failed to realize that, to promote efficiency of the economy, not only must the firms compete with one another, but the management of each competing firm also needs to motivate its employees.

Human capitalism is a confirmation of what's right with Karl Marx, who argued a century and a half ago that cooperation is vital to build a just economic society. At the same time it is an enterprise system designed to avoid the failing of his theory by blending cooperation with competition and diffusing power among groups affiliated with the firm instead of concentrating it in one group.

Management in each country functions in the context of a prevailing economic system. The principles of the system, therefore, condition what management can and cannot do. In the success of human capitalism is the proof that the adversarial relations that often plague American firms are not an inevitable consequence of American culture, but have a systemic root in traditional capitalism itself.

Human capitalism is a little parable on the Aristotelian logic of dichotomy. According to the logic business transactions take place *either* through market *or* within organizations, the firms *either* compete *or* cooperate with each other, and people are *either* individualistic *or* group oriented. Human capitalism reveals that business can be efficiently executed through organized market, competitive cooperation can enhance productivity of the firms, and the same rational people may be individualistic and group oriented, depending on circumstances.

Suppose there is a company that apparently has no organization chart and where workers do not bother with the manual, decide what to do by themselves, and often rotate jobs to be generalists rather than seasoned specialists. While the management textbook will likely declare such a company to be an easy candidate for bankruptcy, we have seen that the firms with these attributes—the attributes of human capitalism—can be thriving, profitable, and highly cohesive organizations.

The strength of America as a nation lies in its willingness to embrace diverse values and experiment with new ideas, in its pragmatism, and in its traditional belief in communitarianism. Human capitalism is an alternative philosophy of management that is perfectly adaptable to American culture.

Neither a quick fix nor a new management technique, human capitalism is a way of looking at the workplace that can be adopted by any society. Japan has shown that it can be the basis for organizing and managing large, complex, and technologically advanced corporations. But its ethos is applicable to all firms, large and small, industrial or nonindustrial.

Human capitalism is what Pete Harman of Kentucky Fried Chicken unwittingly summed up when he said, "You know, at a private company, you don't have to be greedy. You can share it with your good people, and it all comes back to you."

Finally, the lesson of human capitalism for America was vicariously stated in 1988 by Joseph Duffey, chancellor of the University of Massachusetts, when he wrote: "[W]e must recognize that human capital is our greatest competitive potential. The talents of inventors, engineers, managers, and skilled workers will remain our best hope for economic achievement. Our ability to compete hinges on the ability to take advantage of a creative, well-trained labor force. Business and government should see workers as an asset, and not simply as a cost of production. Part of the secret of enhanced productivity lies in making people feel that they are valued members of the economic community."

APPENDIX

TABLE I   INTERNATIONAL COMPARISONS OF LABOR PRODUCTIVITY, 1960–1988
(Average Annual Growth Rate of Volume of Output per Employee in the Business Sector) (%)

	Starting Year	Through 1973	1974–79	1980–85	1986–88
Japan	1960	9.7	3.9	3.1	3.0
U.S.	1962	2.2	0.9	0.9	1.5
W. Germany	1962	5.0	3.6	2.3	2.2
France	1963	5.8	3.1	2.5	2.3
U.K.	1961	3.5	1.1	2.7	1.7
Italy	1960	6.9	2.3	1.4	2.4
Canada	1966	2.8	2.3	1.8	1.0
Average for 20 OECD countries		4.4	2.0	1.7	1.8

Source: Organization for Economic Cooperation and Development.

TABLE II   **LABOR PRODUCTIVITY BY SECTOR IN JAPAN AND THE U.S., 1960–1985**
(Average Annual Growth Rate: %)

	1960–73		1974–85	
	Manufacturing	*Services*	*Manufacturing*	*Services*
Japan	9.5	7.9	6.1	2.8
U.S.	5.5	3.1	3.0	1.3

Source: Organization for Economic Cooperation and Development.

◻

TABLE III   **"YES" ANSWERS TO THE QUESTION "DO YOU THINK IT NECESSARY FOR RANK AND FILE WORKERS TO HAVE A VOICE IN MANAGEMENT?" 1977**
(% of Workers Answering Yes)

	Men	*Women*
19 years old and younger	87.6	78.9
20–24	90.8	85.0
25–29	89.9	82.4
30–34	90.1	79.1
35–39	92.9	79.5
40–44	90.5	78.0
45–54	87.5	78.0
55 and older	81.3	61.7
All ages	90.0	81.7

Source: Ministry of Labor, *Survey on Communication between Labor and Management* (Tokyo, 1978).

TABLE IV	BONUS PAYMENT AMOUNTS IN TERMS OF THE MONTHLY BASIC EARNINGS EQUIVALENT, 1973–1978		
	30+ Employees	*100+ Employees*	*1,000+ Employees*
1973	3.56	5.28	5.9
1974	3.59	5.28	5.8
1975	3.38	4.95	5.2
1976	3.50	4.99	5.0
1977	3.43	4.90	5.2
1978	3.43	4.90	5.1

Source: Ministry of Labor and Japan Productivity Center.

❑

TABLE V	MONTHLY SEPARATION RATES OF WORKERS IN MANUFACTURING INDUSTRIES: JAPAN AND THE U.S., 1955–1980 (%)	
	Japan	*U.S.*
1955	1.8	3.3
1960	2.1	4.3
1965	2.3	4.1
1970	2.3	4.1
1973	2.0	4.6
1974	1.9	4.8
1975	1.7	4.1
1976	1.5	3.8
1977	1.5	3.8
1978	1.4	3.9
1979	1.4	4.0
1980	1.4	4.0

Sources: Ministry of Labor, *Maigetsu Kinro Tokei Chosa,* and Bureau of Labor Statistics, *Monthly Labor Review*.

Appendix

TABLE VI   OWNERSHIP STRUCTURE BY ENTERPRISE GROUP
                (1974–1982 Average) (%)

	Shareholdings by			
	Financial Institutions	*Nonfinancial Corporations*	*Individual Investors*	*Foreign Residents, etc.*
Mitsui	37.0	29.3	30.9	2.8
Mitsubishi	39.6	22.7	34.7	3.0
Sumitomo	34.8	32.0	30.8	2.4
Fuji	37.1	23.4	36.0	3.5
DKB	41.2	21.9	33.5	3.4
Sanwa	40.2	22.1	35.3	2.4

Source: Iwao Nakatani, "The Economic Role of Financial Corporate Grouping," in Masahiko Aoki (ed.), *The Economic Analysis of the Japanese Firm* (N.Y.: North-Holland, 1984), p. 234.

◻

TABLE VII   SIX MAJOR ENTERPRISE GROUPS, 1985

	Number of Corporations in Presidents' Club	*Intragroup Shareholding (%)*	*Intragroup Bank Finance (%)*
Mitsui	24	17.9	21.2
Mitsubishi	28	25.2	22.4
Sumitomo	21	25.0	27.7
Sanwa	44	16.8	20.3
Fuyo	29	15.8	18.4
DKB	47	13.3	12.1

Source: The Oriental Economist, *Kigyo Keiretsu Soran 1987.*

Appendix

TABLE VIII   INCOME DISTRIBUTION BY COUNTRY
(Gini Coefficient)

	Before Tax	After Tax
Japan	0.335	0.316
Sweden	0.346	0.302
W. Germany	0.396	0.383
U.S.	0.404	0.381
OECD average	0.366	0.350

Source: M. Sawyer, *Income Distribution in OECD Countries* (Paris: OECD, 1976).

Note: A smaller (larger) Gini coefficient implies a more (less) equal income distribution.

TABLE IX   CLASS PERCEPTIONS OF JAPANESE HOUSEHOLDS
(May 1988)

Belong to	%
Upper class	0.5
Upper middle class	6.9
Middle middle class	52.8
Lower middle class	29.2
Lower class	7.6
Don't know	3.0

Source: Prime Minister's Office, Japan.

TABLE X   RATE OF UNEMPLOYMENT BY COUNTRY (%)

	1983	1984	1985	1986	1987
Japan	2.6	2.7	2.6	2.8	2.8
U.S.	9.5	7.4	7.1	6.9	6.1
U.K.	12.9	13.1	13.5	11.5	10.4
France	8.8	9.9	10.3	10.4	10.6
W. Germany	9.1	9.1	9.3	9.0	8.9
Italy	9.9	10.4	10.6	11.5	12.0

Source: Bank of Japan, *Kokusai Hikaku Tokei.*

TABLE XI   MUTUAL PERCEPTION OF MANAGEMENT-LABOR RELATIONS BY MANAGEMENTS AND UNIONS

	Union's Perception (%)	Management's Perception (%)
Condition of management-labor relations		
1 very stable	25.0	37.4
2 stable	67.9	55.3
3 rather stable	6.1	5.1
4 unstable	0.9	1.6
5 N.A.	0.2	0.7
Union's attitude toward management's efforts for productivity gains		
1 very cooperative	54.3	57.2
2 cooperative	44.0	39.5
3 not cooperative	0.7	2.5
4 very uncooperative	0.0	0.9
5 N.A.	0.9	0.3
Union's bargaining power		
1 very strong	5.0	4.6
2 strong	57.6	57.2
3 not strong	31.2	33.0
4 weak	5.0	4.2
5 N.A.	1.3	1.1

Sources: Shakai Keizai Kokumin Kaigi, *Kokumin Kaigi Hakusho* (1988 & 1989).

Note: Based on surveys of 1,600 large, and 150 medium-size, firms conducted by Social and Economic Congress of Japan in 1987 and 1988.

TABLE XII

PERCENTAGE OF ESTABLISHMENTS WITH JOINT
CONSULTATION MACHINERY, 1977

Number of Employees in Firm	Firms with Labor Unions	Firms without Labor Unions
5,000 and more	94.1	67.2
1,000–4,999	90.6	46.3
300–999	82.3	42.4
100–299	69.8	38.0
All firms	82.9	40.3

Source: Ministry of Labor, *Survey on Communication between Labor and Management* (Tokyo, 1978).

TABLE XIII

REAL GNP GROWTH RATE BY COUNTRY
(1975–1987) (%)

	Japan	U.S.	W. Germany	France	U.K.
1975	2.6	− 1.0	− 1.6	0.2	− 0.6
1976	4.8	4.8	5.4	5.2	3.8
1977	5.3	4.6	3.0	3.1	1.1
1978	5.1	5.2	2.9	3.3	3.6
1979	5.2	2.1	4.1	3.2	2.1
1980	4.4	− 0.2	1.4	1.6	− 2.1
1981	3.9	2.0	0.2	1.2	− 0.9
1982	2.8	− 2.5	− 0.6	2.5	1.1
1983	3.2	3.7	1.5	0.7	3.5
1984	5.0	7.0	2.8	1.3	2.1
1985	4.7	3.3	2.1	1.7	3.9
1986	2.5	3.1	2.6	2.1	2.9
1987	4.2	3.1	1.8	2.2	3.6

Source: Bank of Japan, *Kokusai Hikaku Tokei.*

TABLE XIV	NUMBER OF WORKING DAYS LOST THROUGH INDUSTRIAL DISPUTES PER 1,000 EMPLOYEES, SELECTED COUNTRIES, 1955–1980				
	1955–59	*1960–64*	*1965–69*	*1970–74*	*1975–80*
Japan	254	177	107	151	69
U.S.	615	301	513	539	389
U.K.	220	146	175	624	521
France	180	197	163	201	195
Italy	433	932	1,204	1,404	1,434

Source: International Labor Office, *Yearbook of Labor Statistics*.

BIBLIOGRAPHY

Chapter 1

Aoki, Masahiko. *Gendai no Kigyo*. Tokyo: Iwanami, 1985.

Aoki, Masahiko, ed. *The Economic Analysis of the Japanese Firm*. New York: North-Holland, 1984.

Demsetz, Harold. *Ownership, Control and the Firm*. New York: Basil Blackwell, 1988.

Itami, Hiroyuki. *Jinponshugi Kigyo*. Tokyo: Chikuma Shobo, 1987.

Itami, Hiroyuki, with Thomas W. Roehl. *Mobilizing Invisible Assets*. Cambridge, Mass.: Harvard University Press, 1987.

Jackall, Robert, and Henry Levin. *Worker Cooperatives in America*. Berkeley: University of California Press, 1984.

Kagono, Tadao, et al. *Strategic vs. Evolutionary Management*. New York: North-Holland, 1985.

Kawamoto, Ichiro. "Kaisha Ho ni Miru Nihon no Tokushitsu." *Nihon Keizai Kenkyu Senta Kaiho* (November 15, 1983).

Leibenstein, Harvey. *Inside the Firm: the Inefficiencies of Hierarchy*. Cambridge, Mass.: Harvard University Press, 1987.

Nihon Seisansei Hombu. *Hataraku Koto no Ishiki*. Tokyo: Japan Productivity Center, 1989.

Nihon Seisansei Hombu. *Rodo no Ningenka to Seisansei Undo*. Tokyo: Japan Productivity Center, 1988.

Nishiyama, Tadanori. *Nihon wa Shihonshugi dewa nai*. Tokyo: Mikasa Shobo, 1982.

Okumura, Hiroshi. *Hojin Shihon Shugi*. Tokyo: Ochanomizu Shobo, 1984.

Putterman, Louis, ed. *The Economic Nature of the Firm*. New York: Cambridge University Press, 1986.

Shakai Keizai Kokumin Kaigi. *Kokumin Kaigi Hakusho 1987*. Tokyo: Social and Economic Congress of Japan, 1987.

Stephen, Frank H. *The Economic Analysis of Producers' Cooperatives*. New York: St. Martin's Press, 1984.

Tanaka, Hiroshi. *The Human Side of Enterprise*. Philadelphia: University of Pennsylvania Press, 1988.

Thomas, Henk, and Chris Logan. *Mondragon: an Economic Analysis*. London: George Allen & Unwin, 1982.

Chapter 2

Aoki, Masahiko. *Information, Incentives and Bargaining in the Japanese Economy*. New York: Cambridge University Press, 1988.

Aoki, Masahiko, Kazuo Koike, and Iwao Nakatani. *Nihon Kigyo no Keizaigaku*. Tokyo: TBS Buritanika, 1986.

Axelrod, Robert. *The Evolution of Cooperation*. New York: Basic Books, 1984.

Doeringer, P., and M. Piore. *Internal Labor Markets and Manpower Analysis*. Boston: D. C. Heath, 1971.

Heckscher, Charles C. *The New Unionism: Employee Involvement in the Changing Corporation*. New York: Basic Books, 1988.

Imai, Kenichi, Hiroyuki Itami, and Kazuo Koike. *Naibusoshiki no Keizaigaku*. Tokyo: Toyo Keizai Shimpo Sha, 1982.

Koike, Kazuo. *Nihon no Jukuren*. Tokyo: Yuhikaku, 1981.

Levine, Solomon B., and Hisashi Kawada. *Human Resources in Japanese Industrial Development*. Princeton: Princeton University Press, 1980.

Lincoln, James F. *Lincoln's Incentive System*. New York: McGraw-Hill, 1946.

Nihon Seisansei Hombu. *Sahbisu Keizaika to Aratana Roshi no Kadai*. Tokyo: Japan Productivity Center, 1989.

Odaka, Kunio. *Toward Industrial Democracy: Management and Workers in Modern Japan.* Cambridge, Mass.: Harvard University Press, 1975.

Shakai Keizai Kokumin Kaigi. *Kokumin Kaigi Hakusho 1988.* Tokyo: Social and Economic Congress of Japan, 1988.

Shirai, Taishiro, ed. *Contemporary Industrial Relations in Japan.* Madison: University of Wisconsin Press, 1983.

Telser, Lester G. *A Theory of Efficient Cooperation and Competition.* New York: Cambridge University Press, 1987.

Tsusan Sho, *Kigyo Katsuryoku.* Tokyo: Toyo Keizai Shimpo Sha, 1984.

Chapter 3

Comanor, William, and Takahiro Miyao. "The Organization and Relative Productivity of Japanese and American Industry." *Managerial and Decision Economics* (June 1985).

Cyert, R. M., and J. G. March. *A Behavioral Theory of the Firm.* Englewood Cliffs, N.J.: Prentice-Hall, 1963.

Hirschman, A. O. *Exit, Voice and Loyalty.* Cambridge, Mass.: Harvard University Press, 1970.

Imai, Kenichi. *Nihon no Sangyoshakai.* Tokyo: Chikuma Shobo, 1983.

Kagono, Tadao, et al. *Nichi-Bei Kigyo no Keiei Hikaku.* Tokyo: Nihon Keizai Shimbun, 1983.

March, James G., and Herbert A. Simon. *Organization.* New York: John Wiley & Sons, 1958.

McKenzie, Richard B. "On the Methodological Boundaries of Economic Analysis." *Journal of Economic Issues* (Fall 1977).

Monden, Yasuhiro. *Toyota Shisutemu.* Tokyo: Kodansha International, 1985.

Nakamura, Hideichiro. *Nihon Sangyo no Chiteki Katsuryoku.* Tokyo: Toyo Keizai Shimpo Sha, 1985.

Okuda, Kenji. *Nihongata Keiei o Ikasu.* Tokyo: Nihon Seisansei Hombu, 1983.

Tsuda, Shincho. *Nihonteki Keiei no Jinji Senryaku.* Tokyo: Dobunkan, 1987.

Uekusa, Masu. *Sangyososhiki Ron*. Tokyo: Chikuma Shobo, 1985.

Williamson, Oliver E. *Markets and Hierarchies*. New York: The Free Press, 1975.

Yamada, Tamotsu. *Nihonteki Keiei no Keizaigaku*. Tokyo: Chuo Keizai Sha, 1980.

Chapter 4

Allen, G. C. *Japan's Economic Recovery*. New York: Oxford University Press, 1958.

Cohen, Jerome B. *Japan's Postwar Economy*. Bloomington: Indiana University Press, 1958.

Dore, Ronald P. *British Factory, Japanese Factory*. Berkeley: University of California Press, 1973.

Hadley, Eleanor M. *Antitrust in Japan*. Princeton: Princeton University Press, 1970.

Keizai Kikaku Cho, *Sengo Keizai Shi*. Tokyo: Ministry of Finance Printing Office, 1957.

Nakamura, Takafusa. *Gendai no Nihon Keizai*. Tokyo: University of Tokyo Press, 1965.

Okochi, Kazuo, Bernard Karsh and Solomon B. Levine. *Workers and Employers in Japan*. Princeton: Princeton University Press, 1974.

Sakamoto, Fujiyoshi. *Nihon Koyo Shi*. Tokyo: Chuo Keizai Sha, 1977.

Tsusan Sho. *Sengo Keizai Junen Shi*. Tokyo: Shoko Kaikan Shuppan Bu, 1954.

Uchino, Tatsuro. *Japan's Postwar Economy*. Tokyo: Kodansha International, 1983.

Ueno, Hiroya. *Nihon no Keizai Seido*. Tokyo: Nihon Keizai Shimbun Sha, 1978.

Chapter 5

Becker, Gary S. *The Economic Approach to Human Behavior*. Chicago: University of Chicago Press, 1976.

Bennett, John, and Iwao Ishino. *Paternalism in the Japanese*

Economy. Minneapolis: University of Minnesota Press, 1963.

Christopher, Robert C. *The Japanese Mind*. New York: Linden Press, 1983.

Collard, David. *Altruism and Economy, a Study in Non-Selfish Economics*. Oxford: Martin Robertson, 1978.

Dale, Peter N. *The Myth of Japanese Uniqueness*. New York: St. Martin's Press, 1986.

Kahn, Herman. *The Emerging Japanese Superstate*. Englewood Cliffs, N.J.: Prentice-Hall, 1970.

Komai, Hiroshi. *Nihonteki Keiei to Ibunka no Rodosha*. Tokyo: Yuhikaku, 1987.

Morishima, Michio. *Why has Japan "Succeeded"?* New York: Cambridge University Press, 1982.

Mouer, Ross, and Yoshio Sugimoto. *Images of Japanese Society*. London: Routledge & Kegan Paul, 1986.

Nakane, Chie. *Japanese Society*. Berkeley: University of California Press, 1970.

Reischauer, Edwin O. *The Japanese*. Cambridge, Mass.: Harvard University Press, 1978.

Chapter 6

Abegglen, James C. *Management and Worker, the Japanese Solution*. Tokyo: Kodansha International, 1973.

Abegglen, James C., and George Stalk, Jr. *Kaisha, the Japanese Corporation*. New York: Basic Books, 1985.

Clark, Rodney. *The Japanese Company*. New Haven: Yale University Press, 1979.

Hashimoto, M., and J. Raisian. "Employment Tenure and Earnings Profiles in Japan and the United States." *American Economic Review* (September 1985).

Hazama, Hiroshi. "Nihongata Roshikankei no Yukue." *Keieisha* (December 1987).

Iwata, Ryushi. *Nihonteki Keiei Ronso*. Tokyo: Nihon Keizai Shimbun Sha, 1984.

Nakatani, Iwao. *The Japanese Firms in Transition*. Tokyo: Asian Productivity Organization, 1988.

Nikkei Sangyo Shimbun, ed. *Shinka Ron, Nihon no Keiei*. Tokyo: Nihon Keizai Shimbun Sha, 1989.

Noda, Nobuo. *Nihon Kindai Keiei Shi*. Tokyo: Sangyo Noritsu Daigaku Shuppan Bu, 1988.

Okura Sho Chosa Kikaku Ka. *Nihongata Keiei Shisutemu no Shorai*. Tokyo: Ministry of Finance Printing Office, 1984.

Ouchi, William G. *Theory Z*. Reading, Mass.: Addison-Wesley, 1981.

Pascale, Richard Tanner, and Anthony G. Athos. *The Art of Japanese Management*. New York: Simon & Schuster, 1981.

Rodo Sho, ed. *Nihonteki Koyo Kanko no Henka to Tembo*. Tokyo: Ministry of Finance Printing Office, 1987.

Sato, Kazuo, ed. *Industry and Business in Japan*. White Plains, N.Y.: M. E. Sharpe, 1980.

Sato, Kazuo, and Yasuo Hoshino, eds. *The Anatomy of Japanese Business*. Armonk, N.Y.: M. E. Sharpe, 1984.

Taira, Koji. "Japan's Lifetime Employment Revisited." *BEBR Faculty Working Paper* No. 1137. University of Illinois at Urbana-Champaign (April 1985).

Tsuda, Tatsuo. *Ningenshugi Keiei no Kiki*. Tokyo: Daiyamondo Sha, 1989.

Chapter 7

Baba, Masao, and Kimihiro Masamura, eds. *Sangyo Shakai to Nihonjin*. Tokyo: Chikuma Shobo, 1980.

Balogh, Thomas. *The Irrelevance of Conventional Economics*. New York: Liveright Publishing, 1982.

Bowles, Samuel, David M. Gordon, and Thomas E. Weisskopf. *Beyond the Waste Land*. Garden City, N.Y.: Doubleday, 1984.

Bowles, Samuel, and Herbert Gintis. *Democracy and Capitalism*. New York: Basic Books, 1986.

Clayre, Alasdair, ed. *The Political Economy of Cooperation and Participation*. Oxford: Oxford University Press, 1980.

Dore, Ronald P. *Taking Japan Seriously*. Stanford, Calif.: Stanford University Press, 1987.

Flexner, Kurt F. *The Enlightened Society*. Lexington, Mass.: Lexington Books, 1989.

Iida, Tsuneo. *Nihon Keizai wa Doko e Ikunoka*. Kyoto: PHP, 1986.

Keizai Doyukai. *1990 Nendai no Kigyo Keiei*. Tokyo: Japan Committee for Economic Development, 1985.

Namiki, Nobuyoshi, ed. *Nihon Shakai no Tokushitsu*. Tokyo: Nihon Keizai Shimbun Sha, 1981.

Nihon Seisansei Hombu. *Korekara no Keiei Rinen to Sangyojin no Kachikan*. Tokyo: Japan Productivity Center, 1979.

Nikkeiren, *Zennin Sanka Keiei*. Tokyo: Japan Federation of Employers' Associations, 1976.

Nishiyama, Tadanori. *Datsu Shihonshugi Bunseki*. Tokyo: Bunshin Do, 1983.

Odaka, Kunio. *Nihonteki Keiei*. Tokyo: Chuo Koron Sha, 1984.

Williamson, Oliver E. *The Economic Institutions of Capitalism*. New York: Free Press, 1985.

Yoshikawa, Eiichi. *Korekara no Nihongata Jinji Kanri*. Tokyo: Yuhikaku, 1987.

Yoshimori, Ken. *Seio Kigyo no Hasso to Kodo*. Tokyo: Daiyamondo Sha, 1979.

Chapter 8

Berger, Peter L. *The Capitalist Revolution*. New York: Basic Books, 1986.

Galbraith, John Kenneth, and Stanislav Menshikov. *Capitalism, Communism and Coexistence*. Boston: Houghton Mifflin, 1988.

Haitani, Kanji. *Comparative Economic Systems*. Englewood Cliffs, N.J.: Prentice-Hall, 1986.

Katouzian, Homa. *Ideology and Method in Economics*. New York: New York University Press, 1980.

Lodge, George E., and Ezra F. Vogel, eds. *Ideology and National Competitiveness*. Boston: Harvard Business School Press, 1987.

Nakagawa, Yatsuhiro, and Nobumasa Ota, *The Japanese-Style Economic System*. Tokyo: Foreign Press Center, 1981.

Nove, Alec. *The Economics of Feasible Socialism*. London: George Allen & Unwin, 1983.

Okun, Arthur M. *Equality and Efficiency*. Washington, D.C.: The Brookings Institution, 1975.

Schumpeter, Joseph A. *Capitalism, Socialism and Democracy*. New York: Harper & Brothers, 1950.

Ward, Benjamin. *The Ideal Worlds of Economics*. New York: Basic Books, 1979.

Chapter 9

Adizes, Ichak. *Industrial Democracy, Yugoslav Style*. New York: Free Press, 1971.

Andrew, John and William Nordhaus, eds. "The Share Economy: A Symposium." *Journal of Comparative Economics* (December 1986).

Garson, David, ed. *Worker Self-Management in Industry*. New York: Praeger, 1977.

Ireland, Norman J., and Peter J. Law. *The Economics of Labor-Managed Enterprises*. New York: St. Martin's Press, 1982.

Jones, Derek C., and Jan Svejnar, eds. *Participatory and Self-Managed Firms*. Lexington, Mass.: Lexington Books, 1982.

Kuhne, Robert J. *Co-Determination in Business*. New York: Praeger, 1980.

Lawrence, Peter. *Managers and Management in West Germany*. New York: St. Martin's Press, 1980.

Lydall, Harold. *Yugoslav Socialism: Theory and Practice*. Oxford: Clarendon Press, 1984.

Mason, Ronald M. *Participatory and Workplace Democracy*. Carbondale: Southern Illinois University Press, 1982.

Meade, James E. "The Theory of Labor-Managed Firms and of Profit-Sharing." *Economic Journal* (March 1972).

Sik, Ota. *For a Humane Economic Democracy*. New York: Praeger, 1979.

Vanek, Jaroslav. *The Labor-Managed Economy*. Ithaca: Cornell University Press, 1977.

Weitzman, Martin L. *The Share Economy*. Cambridge, Mass.: Harvard University Press, 1984.

Chapter 10

Ampo, Tetsuo. *Nihon Kigyo no Amerika Genchi Seisan*. Tokyo: Toyo Keizai Shimpo Sha, 1988.

Brady, Michael. "Toyota Meets U.S. Auto Workers." *Fortune* (July 9, 1984).

Ishida, Hideo. *Nihon Kigyo no Kokusai Jinji Kanri*. Tokyo: Nihon Rodo Kyokai, 1985.

Johnson, Chalmers. "Japanese-Style Management in America." *California Management Review* (Summer 1988).

Kraan, Louis. "The Japanese are Coming—with Their Own Style of Management." *Fortune* (March 10, 1975).

Lee, Bruce. "Worker Harmony Makes Nummi Work." *The New York Times* (December 25, 1988).

Lee, Sang M., and Gary Schwendiman, eds. *Management by Japanese Systems*. New York: Praeger, 1982.

Lincoln, James F. *Incentive Management*. Cleveland, Ohio: Lincoln Electric Company, 1951.

Matsuno, Saichi, and William A. Stoever. "Japanese Boss, American Employees." *Wharton Magazine* (Fall 1982).

Parker, Mike, and Jane Slaughter. "Behind the Scenes at NUMMI Motors." *The New York Times* (December 4, 1988).

Shigesato, Toshiyuki. "Nihonkigyno no Takokuseki Ka to Roshi Kankei." *Nihon Rodo Kyokai Zasshi* (October 1988).

Shimada, Haruo. *Hyumanueya no Keizaigaku*. Tokyo: Iwanami, 1988.

Starr, Martin, ed. *Global Competitiveness: Getting the U.S. Back on Track*. New York: W. W. Norton, 1988.

INDEX

Absenteeism, 82
Affluence, 94, 109–10, 123
Age-based hierarchy, 104–5
Alienation, 31, 34, 77, 122, 123–24, 128–29, 154
Antimonopoly law, 66, 79
Antitrust laws, 9, 57, 130
Argentina, 86
Art of Japanese Management, The (Pascale and Athos), 166
Athos, Anthony G., 166
Automobile companies
  Japanese, in U.S., 167–74, 176–77
Automobile industry, 58, 83, 84–85, 175

Baťa, Tomáš, 163
Banks, 15, 51, 53, 54, 56, 73, 74, 161
Blue-collar workers, 101, 112–13, 122, 123, 124
Boeing (co.), 166
Bonuses, 23, 103, 112, 113, 156, 187*t*
Burden sharing, 24–25, 110
Bushido, 91

Capital, 12–13, 17, 51, 133, 134, 143, 144–45, 158
  see also Human capital
Capital market, 72–74, 116

Capital/technology-intensive mode of production, 60
Capitalism, 3–5, 9, 20, 116–17, 118, 125, 132, 146, 150, 182
  attempts to reform, 141–57
  competition in, 45
  continuity between traditional and human, 158–59
  and economic reform in Eastern Europe, 141–42
  efficiency/equity trade-off in, 138, 140
  emergence of, in England, 2, 5, 6, 72, 77, 78
  firm in, 10
  human capitalism compared with, 126–40
  and innovation, 58
  ironies and paradoxes of, 135–37
  labor-management power relation in, 41–42, 43, 44
  modeled in neoclassical economics, 87–88
  ownership/control in, 16–18, 114
  private enterprise system, 57
  and socialism, 75–77, 126–30
  sovereignty in, 12–15, 16
  spread of, 96, 180
  state-guided, 57
  values in, 6–7
  view of socialism, 130–34

"Capitalism with a human face," ix, 159
Capitalist class, 112, 113
Capitalistic firm, 8–9, 21, 26, 35
  managerial system, 127
  and unemployment, 120
Central economic planning, 127, 143
  see also Planned economy
Cheese Board (co.), 22
China, 126, 141, 151
Chrysler Corporation, 152
Class consciousness, 8, 169
  England, 178, 179
Class perceptions
  of Japanese households, 189*t*
Class structure, 112–13
Class struggle, 98, 130
Codetermination, 151–54
Cold War, 66, 76
Collective bargaining, 41, 42, 44, 66, 68, 70, 106, 176
Command economy, 127
Communication, 181
Communication system, 169–70
Communism, 76, 77, 151
Company union, 42, 68, 106
Compensation, 16, 18, 23, 24, 37–38, 109, 156, 171–72
  under JSMS, 102–5
  seniority and, 29, 100
  see also Executive salaries; Wages
Competition, 1, 2, 7, 9, 47, 48, 50, 52, 60, 93, 138
  and cooperation, 140, 182
  free, 136, 138, 182
  interfirm, 8, 29–30, 41, 42, 45, 62, 140
  mixing with control, 147–51
  and organization, 56–57
  patterns of, 45–46
  among workers, 28, 45, 62, 100
  see also Market competition
Competitive egalitarianism, 26–46, 62
Confucianism, 91–92

Consensual management system, 136–37
Control, 16–21, 147–51
Cooperation, 1, 2, 8, 9, 21, 46, 61, 74, 93, 97, 180
  and competition, 140, 182
  emphasis on, 170, 182
  labor-management, 69, 70–71, 98–99, 177
  in organization, 47, 50
  among workers, 27, 28, 35
Cooperative firms, 53, 159–65
Cooperative relations
  enterprise groups, 51, 54–56
  firm/subcontractor, 51–53
Cooperativeness (cultural trait), 69
Corporate ownership, 7, 8–9, 10–11, 19–20, 70, 151–52
Corporate shareholding, 133
Corporatism, 57
Costs/benefits, 29–30, 43–44, 94
Čuba, Ing F., 163
Culture, 80–95
  and economic theory, 86–88
  and human capitalism, 2–3, 104–5
  and JSMS, 99–100, 165–66
  and management systems, 96–98
Culture model, 2–3, 80–86, 91–92
Czechoslovakia, 142

Debt financing, 15, 18, 73, 74, 161, 172
Decision making, 9, 24, 30–34, 146
  centralized, vertical, 127
  consensual, 1, 8, 11, 24, 97, 109, 110
  decentralized, 32–34, 42, 52–53, 60–61, 102, 170
  hierarchical, 30–32
Defense Science Policy Board, 59
Delta Airlines (co.), 166
Demoralization, 11, 31, 32, 182
Dichotomy, 182–83
Discipline, 35, 36, 40, 41, 140
Diseconomies of scale, 51, 57, 73
Division of labor, 21, 26, 31

Dore, Ronald, 180
Duffey, Joseph, 183

Eastern Europe, 126, 129, 141–42, 151
Eastman Kodak (co.), 166
Economic change, 108–9, 110–11, 118
Economic freedom, 136–37, 151
Economic functionalism, 21
Economic growth, 2, 3–4, 71, 84, 89, 98, 107–9, 131, 132–33, 165
Economic organization firm as, 21–23, 47
Economic philosophy, 10
Economic power, 134, 146
Economic reform, 75, 150–51, 157
  misguided, 141–42
  post-WWII, 66–67
Economic statistics, 139
Economic systems, 3–4, 78, 132, 182
  new, ix, 1–5, 6
  people-oriented, 181–82
  power in, 146–47
  transfer of, 180–82
  values and principles in, 3, 6–7, 96, 97
Economic theory, 86–88
Economics, 3–4, 10, 86–88
  see also Neoclassical economics
Economy, ix–x, 108–9, 114
  mixed, 3, 4, 138
  see also Planned economy
Efficiency (economic), 21–22, 24, 32, 48, 82, 129, 153, 182
  of capitalism, 131
  economic freedom and, 136–37
  in enterprise groups, 57
  and equity, 138–40
  of market economy, 150, 158
  political democracy and, 145–46
  welfare and, 119
Egalitarian society, 112–15
Egalitarianism, 2, 38, 77, 104–5, 171, 175, 179
  competitive, 26–46, 62

EI (Employee Involvement), 176
Employment security, 29, 58, 98–99, 100, 101, 156, 170
Enterprise groups, 51, 53–57, 61, 73, 74, 116, 117
  competition among, 8, 45
  major, 188*t*
  ownership structure by, 188*t*
  Presidents' Clubs, 54
Enterprise system(s), 96, 113–14, 140
Enterprise union(s), 41–44, 66, 67–69, 97, 162, 174, 179
  and innovation, 59–60
  in JSMS, 105–7
Enterprise welfare, 97, 118–20
Entrepreneurship, 62–63
Equality, 23, 77
Equity, 7, 138–40
Equity financing, 18, 65
ESOP (Employee Stock Ownership Plan), 157
Evaluation criteria, 36
Executive salaries, 23, 24, 38, 39, 115, 171–72
  gap between workers' and, 9, 112, 113, 124
Executives, 11, 38–39

Fair Trade Commission, 57
Family-owned firm, 12, 17, 69–70
Feudalism, 82, 92, 114
Firings, 37, 100, 101, 171
Firm(s), 18, 47, 58, 74, 124–25
  as economic/social organization, 74, 122, 125, 129–30, 153
  efficiency in, 138–39
  family-owned, 12, 17, 69–70
  independent, 56
  in market socialism, 145
  nature of, 6–12
  neoclassical theory of, 4, 87–88
  overseas, 109
  people-oriented, 159–65
  as quasi-familial organization, 97, 99

see also Capitalistic firm; Humanistic firm
Fletcher Jones Company, 162–63, 164
Flexible manufacturing systems (FMS), 59
Ford, Henry, 176
Ford Motor Company, 176
Foreign firms in Japan, 109–10
Foreign investment, 109, 167
Fraser, Douglas, 152
Free-enterprise economies, 58, 87
Free-enterprise system, 58, 87, 90, 127, 131
Free market, 9, 114, 116
  see also Market competition
Freedom, 77, 135–37, 151, 161
  individual, 6–7, 58, 116
  occupational, 128
  organized, 117–19
Fuji Heavy Industries, 56
Fujitsu (co.), 63

General Motors (GM), 152, 170
Germany, 74–75
Golden, Jeremy, 179
Gorbachev, Mikhail, 141
Great Britain, 75, 96, 177–80, 181
Great Depression, 68, 75, 138, 159
Grievances, 37, 42, 170
Gross national product, 139
  growth rate of real, by country, 191*t*
Group-oriented enterprise, 159–65, 182–83
Groupism, 88–92, 95

Haedads Coop, 160
Harman, Pete, 183
Harmony, 61, 83–84, 85
Heavy industry, 99–100, 108
Hewlett-Packard (co.), 166
Hitachi (co.), 63
HMC (Hitachi Magnetics Corporation), 25
Hodgson, James D., 175–76

Homogeneity, 85–86
Honda, Soichiro, 63
Honda Motors (co.), 63, 72
  U.S. plant, 168, 171, 174, 176
Housing, 103, 119, 138, 149–50
Howard, Diane, 173
Human capital, 1, 12, 27–28, 33, 34, 60, 183
Human capitalism, 1–5, 57, 63, 107, 140, 158–59, 164–65, 178, 182–83
  and American workers, 168–74, 175–76
  birth of, 74–76
  comparison with capitalism and socialism, 126–40
  and culture, 104–5
  disadvantages of, 33–34, 38, 40–41, 61–63
  evolution of, 64–79
  future of, 76–79
  in Great Britain, 177–80
  implications of, 112–25
  and JSMS, 96–97, 110–11
  parts of, not transferable to other countries, 165–67, 168, 179
  principles of, 10, 77
  transfer of, 2, 165–67, 180–82
  universality of, 3, 78, 96–97, 158–83
Human needs, 122–23
Human resources, 1, 10, 19, 114, 124, 128, 133, 158
  allocation of, 98, 105, 120
Humanistic enterprise system, 1, 6–25, 73–74, 152
  American prototype, 168, 174
  enterprise union in, 67, 69
  freedom in, 116–17, 136–37
  groupism and, 92–93
  values in, 74–76
Humanistic firm(s), 4, 16, 18–19, 53, 101, 103, 113, 117, 125
  authority structure, 20–21
  decision making, 32–34

differences from worker cooperatives, 161–62
distinct from traditional capitalistic firm, 1–2
incentive system, 35–38
inherent problems in, 61–63
innovation in, 58–61, 63
joint sovereignty in, 154
and labor market, 26–28
labor organization in, 42–44
management, 20–21, 39–41, 96–97
and organized market, 51–53
self-interest in, 93–95
welfare provisions, 119–20
Hungary, 142

Iaccoca, Lee, 90
Ideology, 74–76, 128–29, 161
in capitalism/socialism mutual images, 130, 131–34
and freedom, 115–16
Incentive management, 159–65
Incentive Management (Lincoln), 164
Incentive system, 34–38, 104
Income distribution, 77, 112, 124, 140
by country, 189*t*
Incomes policy, 148, 149
Incorporation, 133–34
Individualism, 45, 129, 161, 173, 182–83
vs. groupism, 88–92
Industrial Bank, 56
Industrial democracy, 77, 145–46, 152, 153, 162, 169–70, 175
Industrial Patriotic Society, 65–66
Industrial relations, 67, 70, 84, 107, 174–77
working days lost through disputes, 192*t*
Industrial Revolution, 78, 131
Industrialism, 89, 118, 121–23
Industrialization, 82, 88, 122
Inflation, 148, 149, 154, 156

Information, 47–48, 49, 53, 102, 179
Innovations, 58–61, 62–63
"Invisible hand," 45
Italy, 75, 86, 96

Jakimar, Jay, 59
Japan, 181
class perceptions, 189*t*
impact of U.S. occupation on, 64–67, 70
labor productivity by sector, 186*t*
Japanese-style management system (JSMS), 3, 24, 65, 71–72, 96–111, 178
core elements of, 97
evolution of, 72
not transportable, 165–67
Job applicants, 100, 168–69, 179
Job change, 82, 100, 101, 109–10
Job rotation, 28, 36, 72, 170
Job-security rule, 59–60
see also Employment security
Job sharing, 119
Job specialization, 31, 35, 72, 170
Johnson, Lyndon B., 148
Joint consultation machinery, 106
percentage of establishments with, 191*t*
Joint management-worker sovereignty, 12–16, 19
Joint stock company, 133–34
JSMS. *See* Japanese-style management system (JSMS)
JZD Agrokombinát Slušovice, 163

Kanban system, 84–85
Kawasaki (co.), 63
Korea, 86, 91
Kyocera (co.), 63, 72

Labor, 12, 17, 24–25, 133, 134
Labor force. *See* Work force
Labor-intensive mode of production, 60, 156

Labor-management relations, 41–43,
79, 107, 178
in codetermination, 152–54
conflict of interest in, 153–54
cooperative, 69, 70–71, 98–99,
177
mutual perception of, 190*t*
postwar, 68–69, 76
prewar, 64–65, 113
U.S., 82–83
Labor market, 120
external, 26, 27, 102, 116, 169
Labor market, internalized, 11, 16,
26–30, 36, 37, 60, 65, 94, 109,
136
costs in, 29
and economic change, 109
and seniority-based wage system,
103–4
Labor mobility, interfirm, 16, 26–
27, 82, 98, 101, 104, 109–10,
136
Labor movements, 106–7
Labor organization, 41–44, 67–69
humanistic, 176–77
Labor productivity
international comparisons, 185*t*
by sector (Japan and U.S.), 186*t*
see also Productivity
Labor transfers, 100, 109–10
in enterprise groups, 24, 51
Laissez-faire, 89–90, 138
Layoffs, 24, 44, 71, 108
see also Minimum-layoff policy
Lee, Bruce, 172
Lifetime employment, 70–71, 167,
169
Lifetime-employment system, 65,
71, 82, 97, 98, 99–102, 104,
105, 107, 109, 110
Lincoln, James F., 163, 164
Lincoln Electric (co.), 163–64
Loyalty to firm, 82–83, 93, 97

MacArthur, Douglas, 67
Management, 1, 38–41, 43, 127,
182

in capitalist firm, 9, 13, 14, 17,
20, 58
in codetermination, 153–54
consensual and participatory, 98,
162
hierarchical structure of, 162
humanistic, 8, 11–12, 18–19, 33,
181
in market socialism, 143, 145, 146
perception of labor-management
relations, 190*t*
philosophy of, 180, 183
and sovereignty, 15–16
workers' views on worker participation in, 186*t*
see also Incentive management
Management autonomy, 40–41, 73–
74, 172
Management system(s), 3, 96–99,
127, 137
American, 71–72, 102, 174–77
Japanese-owned companies in
other countries, 172–74, 178–
80
see also Japanese-style management system (JSMS)
Management training, 169
Managerial revolution, 69–72
Managers, 40, 42, 70
Manufacturing firms, 51–53, 54
Manufacturing industries
separation rates: Japan and U.S.,
187*t*
Marginal-productivity theory of
wage, 38–39
Marginalist school, 87
Market(s), 49, 63
see also Organized market
Market competition, 7, 41, 45, 58,
127, 139, 140, 182
and economic control, 141
and efficiency, 158
and enterprise groups, 56–57
in market socialism, 143
Market economy, 9, 33, 147–51
Market socialism, 142–47, 152

Market structure, 87, 88
Marx, Karl, 6, 64, 76, 131, 150, 182
Materialistic concerns, 11–12
Matsushita, Konosuke, 63
Matsushita Electric (co.), 28, 63, 72
Means of production
 ownership of, 7, 17, 114, 130,
 134, 135
Meiji Japan, 91, 93
Merit pay, 37–38, 102
Middle class, 112, 113
Minimum-layoff policy, 24–25, 60,
 71, 99, 107–8, 119–20, 170–
 71, 179
Mismanagement, 40–41
Mitsubishi (co.), 63
Mitsui holding company, 65
Mondragon Cooperative Federation,
 160
Monopolistic competition, 48
Monopoly, 29–30, 41, 52, 56, 78,
 130, 136, 140
Monopoly capitalism, 64–65, 66, 67
Morale, 37–38
Morita, Akio, 63
Motivation, 11, 18, 22, 23–24, 44,
 47, 48, 182
Mutual consultation system, 106,
 191*t*
Mutual stockholding, 7, 15, 18, 53,
 73

Narita International Airport, 84
National income, 139
National Labor Relations Act, 177
National Science Foundation, 59
NEC (co.), 63
Neoclassical economics, 4, 17, 38,
 45–46, 87–88, 98
Networking, 50, 51, 61
New Japan Steel (co.), 63, 110
Nissan (co.), 56, 63, 171
Nonideological society, 74–76
Nummi (co.), 36
 U.S. plant, 168–73, 174, 175–77

Oil crisis, 24, 108, 148
Organization, 47–63
Organized freedom, 115–17
Organized market(s), 8, 47–53, 54,
 79, 88, 161, 182
Ouchi, William G., 166
Ownership, 12, 15, 16–21, 70
 see also Corporate ownership
Ownership structure
 by enterprise group, 188*t*

Parker, Mike, 172–73
Participation, 74, 170, 176, 180
Pascale, Richard Tanner, 166
Patents, 59
Pecuniary income, 23, 115
Peer pressure, 34, 36
Pensions, 55, 113
People orientation, 1, 2, 9–10, 76,
 78, 111, 157, 175, 181
People-oriented firms, 159–65
Personnel department, 102
Personnel transfers, 100, 109–10,
 119
Planned economy, 10, 147–51
Plywood Cooperatives, 160, 162
Poland, 86, 131, 142
Political democracy, 66, 142, 145–
 46, 152–53
Political freedom, 151
Power, 78, 146–47
 distribution of, 134–35, 182
 seniority and, 105
Pragmatism, 75, 76, 183
Price/wage controls, 148–51
Private enterprise system, 12, 57,
 138
Private property rights, 7, 16–17
Procter & Gamble (co.), 166
Product development, 60–61
Productivity, 10, 11, 44, 59–60, 77,
 103–4, 107, 182, 183
 compensation gap and, 124
 decision making and, 33, 34
 enterprise groups, 55, 57
 incentives and, 35–36

joint, 115
and labor mobility, 26, 27, 29
Profit making, 11, 12
Profit maximization, 4, 11, 18, 40,
56, 138–39
Profit-sharing, 9, 23
Promotion, 36–37, 40, 62, 100, 107,
110, 113
Psychic rewards, 23, 38, 39, 115
Psychological satisfaction, 11, 22–
24, 122–23
Public sector, 138

Quality, 169, 170, 173, 179, 180
workers' responsibility for, 174,
175, 176

Rational behavior
self-interest and, 92–95
Recession(s), 24–25, 119
Recruitment, 11, 109, 110
Rent control, 149–50
Research and development, 59, 60–
61
Resource allocation, 6, 144
optimum, 138
supply and demand, 147
with wage/price controls, 148–51
Retirement, 99, 100, 104
Rice farming, 84, 91
Russian Revolution, 130–31

Salaries, 23
see also Executive salaries
Sanyo (co.), 63
Scandinavia, 152
Scott Bader Commonwealth, 160
Second-career opportunities, 100
Self-interest, 92–95
Semiconductor industry, 58, 59
Seniority, 104, 105, 110, 156
and compensation, 100, 102
Seniority-based wage system, 97,
98, 100, 102–5, 167, 179
and economic growth, 109, 110
Seniority pay, 37, 38

Separation rates
manufacturing industries: Japan
and U.S., 187*t*
Severance pay, 55, 73
Share economy, 154–57
Share Economy, The (Weitzman),
155–57
Sharing, 2, 8, 19, 21–25, 35, 74,
94, 97, 111, 140, 162
Sharp (co.), 63
Shirking, 34–35, 36, 41, 101
Singapore, 57
Skilled workers, 65, 100
Skills, 101, 117, 168
Skills transfer, 27, 29
Slaughter, Jane, 172–73
Small-group activity, 32–33, 180
Smith, Adam, 4–5, 45, 64, 76, 87,
92, 118, 132, 158, 182
Social change, 109–10, 113–14
Social status, 39, 115
Social structure, 113–14, 118
Socialism, 1–2, 3–4, 7, 16, 58, 78,
113, 116, 146
attempts to reform, 141–57
and capitalism, 75–77, 126–30
firm in, 10
efficiency/equity trade-off, 138,
139–40
human capitalism compared with,
126–40, 158–59
view of capitalism, 130–34
welfare issues in, 119
see also Market socialism
Socialist regimes, 126, 131, 141–42
economic reform, 143–47, 151
Sony Corporation, 63, 72
Sovereignty, 9, 12–13, 14, 114, 129
firm, 1, 9–10
joint management-worker, 12–16,
19
Soviet Union, 76, 113, 141–42
Stagflation, 108, 148, 149
State (the), 58, 78, 118
economic role, 10, 11, 13, 90
Steel industry, 68, 72, 83

Stock market, 72–73
Stockholders, 7, 8–9, 13, 15, 20–21, 40, 127, 151
  see also Mutual stockholding
Strikes, 71, 84, 107
Subcontracting, 51–53, 54, 57
Supervision, 34–35, 36, 37
Sweden, 86
Switzerland, 86

Taiwan, 57
Teamwork, 27, 28, 35–36, 93, 171, 178
Technology, 6, 58–60, 61
Telecommunications industry, 58, 59
Thailand, 91
Theory Z (Ouchi), 166
3M (co.), 166
Thurley, Keith, 178
Toshiba (co.), 28, 63
Toyo Kogyo (co.), 24–25
Toyota Motor Corporation, 63, 85
Training, 27, 28, 60, 65, 169
Training costs, 33, 169
Transaction cost(s), 48–49
Trevor, Malcolm, 178–79

UAW, 25, 170, 172, 174, 177
Unemployment, 94, 119–20, 154, 156, 159
Unemployment compensation, 120, 138, 147
Unemployment rate
  by country, 190*t*
Unionism, 67–69, 76
Unions, 10, 14, 17, 41, 42, 58, 127, 137, 146
  adversarial vs. internalized, 176–77
  British, 178
  contracts of, 43, 44
  enterprise-based, 65–66
  industrial, 67, 68, 105, 106
  perception of labor-management relations, 190*t*
  role in JSMS, 105–7, 174

United Airlines (co.), 166
United States, 71, 76, 81, 96, 122, 152, 161
  corporate ownership/control in, 19–20
  education system, 160
  freedom in, 115–17, 128
  homogeneity in, 85–86
  industrial relations in, 174–77
  Japanese auto companies in, 167–74, 175, 176–77
  labor productivity by sector, 186*t*
  lesson of human capitalism for, 183
  managerial revolution, 70, 71–72
  occupation of Japan, 64–67, 70, 74, 76, 113–14
  as superpower, 132, 180, 181
Utopianism, 76–77

Value added, 8, 13, 14, 17, 23, 60, 140
Values, ix, 6–7, 12
Vertical command system, 9, 30–31, 33, 127, 128

Wage system, 8, 23, 103, 154–56
  see also Seniority-based wage system
Wages, 17, 44, 62, 121, 137, 154
  in enterprise-group firms, 55
  internalized labor market, 29–30
  in Japanese-owned plants in U.S., 171
  marginal-productivity theory of, 38–39
  and national income, 139
Wagner Act of 1935 (U.S.), 68
Wealth of Nations, The (Smith), 4–5, 87, 132
Weitzman, Martin, 155–57
Welfare, 7, 87, 89, 130, 138, 161
  see also Enterprise welfare
Welfare state, 118–19
West Germany, 96, 152–53
Western culture, 2, 75–76, 88

White, Michael, 178–79
White-collar workers, 101, 112–13, 122
Work as disutility, 120–22, 123
Work ethic, 83, 89, 93–95, 122, 146, 162
  Great Britain, 178, 180
Work force, 33–34, 37, 102, 151, 183
  integrated, productive, 136, 168
  internalized, 53, 62, 93, 117
  percent under JSMS, 97
Work rules, 44, 137, 166
Worker cooperatives, 159–65
Workers, 33–34, 153–54
  American, in Japanese-owned plants in U.S., 168–73, 175–76
  in capitalism, 9, 10, 13, 14, 17, 21, 31–32, 127–28
  costs/benefits, 29–30, 43–44
  in culture model, 81–82
  in human capitalism, 8, 11, 12, 18–19, 114–15
  long-term employment, 11, 29, 61, 103, 104
  loyalty to firm, 82, 83, 93, 97
  in market socialism, 143, 145, 146, 147
  responsibility assumed by, 170, 174, 175, 176
  under socialism, 10, 127–28
  and sovereignty, 15–16
  status of, 123–24, 125
  view of worker participation in management, 186*t*
Working days lost
  industrial disputes, 192*t*
Workplace, 120–25, 181, 183
World War II, 65–66, 68, 69, 74

YKK (co.), 63, 72, 113
Yugoslavia, 86, 131, 143–47, 152
Yutai (courageous retirement) system, 104

Zaibatsu system, 64, 65, 66–67, 70, 112

About the Author

Robert S. Ozaki received his B.A. from Ohio Wesleyan University and an M.A. and Ph.D. in economics from Harvard University. A member of Phi Beta Kappa and Omicron Chi Epsilon, he has served on the advisory editorial board of *The Journal of Asian Studies* and as a Fulbright-Hayes lecturer in Japan, where he was born and grew up. His works have been published in the United States, Japan, Australia, Italy, India, and Korea. At present he is a professor of economics at California State University, Hayward.